TRUE NORTH

LIVING & LEADING ON PURPOSE

DONALD PAUL WILDER

CONTENTS

Printed in the United States of America

First Printing, 2021

ISBN ebook 978-0578844732

ISBN softcover 13-978-0578844718

For bulk orders www.DPaulWilder.com

DEDICATION

The greatest influencers/leaders in my life from birth to now. Donald Wayne Wilder and Sherrie Faye Wilder raised me with love, diligence, integrity, and a love for God's Word. My grandfather, Paul Franklin Wilder, taught me to work hard and to have a strong grip, a strong stance, and a gentle heart. Amy Justice Wilder, my wife, who knows my every success and every failure and loves me anyway. My children, Caleb, Natalie, Joshua, and Timothy for whom this work was originally done. There is no greater motivation to become a better leader than becoming a dad. Henry Grady Justice, my father in-law and friend, who reminded me to always find a way to finish the job and to BYOJ (bring your own joy.) I really miss our morning coffee, Henry! My pastor of 18 years and friend forever, Gene Evans, who found ways to see the best in his "flock" and taught me to live like the Bible is true. My current pastor and friend, James Cordell, who continues to influence me to teach everyday people how to simply live for God and to intentionally develop leaders. May their influence and contributions feed this project in ways that "pay it forward" and provide good fruit to all our accounts.

INTRODUCTION

Leadership is such a popular term. Intending to avoid just tackling a trendy term, Jim Collins, articulates his desire to avoid the topic of leadership in his best seller, *Good To Great: Why Some Companies Make the Leap...and Others Don't.* He and his research team discover; however, that the data will not allow him to write about companies that perform ten times better than market average without discussing what he calls the "Level 5 leader." My take on his description of the Level 5 leader is the secret sauce (not so secret since his book was published in 2000) of great determination to ensure the company accomplishes its mission and a personal humility that does not care who gets the credit. I have certainly oversimplified a great book, but I would encourage the reading of this bestseller. Leadership really does matter, and it starts with leading yourself. Everyone is a leader. Leadership is easily interpreted based on titles and position; the very fact that we all have a name that begins with a capital letter means that we are, at minimum, in ownership of the title _____ (insert your name here.) Your own leadership matters, and the better you lead you, the more likely it is your sphere of leadership influence will expand.

Therefore, as you lead people who matter to do things that matter, you have already begun self-leadership by reading a book focused on intentional and replicable principle-centered leadership. Throughout this journey, we will utilize words of people who have stated principles and ideas articulating for us truths that serve as foundational realities on which to build this legacy of leadership. We stand on the shoulders of other great men and women while becoming one of those great leaders ourselves.

Imagine growing up, a simple fisherman in a small Jewish community, struggling to make a living as your hometown is occupied by the Roman Empire. Soldiers patrolled the streets and docks regularly to help keep order and facilitate the collection of taxes to sustain such a great empire. You are stressed out because you worked hard all night catching nothing, and are now cleaning your nets by the shore in the hopes you will catch some sleep before having to go out again. While finishing up this great chore of cleaning your nets, a man who has garnered a good crowd is being pressed toward your location, enters your fishing vessel, requests that you push away from the shore a little, sits down and begins to deliver words you have never heard. You and your brother, who share the same trade of fishing, are not sure why you so easily went along with this trespasser's plan, but there seems to be no harm in loaning the boat to the unknown person. This uninvited visitor finishes speaking to the crowd and turns to you, telling you to launch back out into the deep and let down the nets you so strenuously cleaned. In His command is the promise of a big catch. You tell him that you've fished all night and caught nothing. After all, you are a fisherman and there are no indications that he is; however, you respond by saying, "if you insist." You go out and do as commanded and the miraculous surprise of a lifetime occurs. You haul in such a big catch that your nets are breaking under the load and you need help from other ships to collect the great harvest of so many fish. Suddenly you are overwhelmed with joy and condemnation all at the same time. You have never caught that many fish. They lined the bottom of your boat making it difficult for you to break down in humility and kneel before this amazing orator and fisherman. You finally bow down and declare that you are not worthy of His intervention in your life; however, He asks you and two of your partners to follow Him so he can make you fishers of men. You have no idea what's in store, but you know this Man is someone special and you are willing to follow His lead.

Perhaps you already recognize this story from the fifth chapter of the book of Luke in the Bible. Peter is the fisherman and he begins a journey that sees miracle after miracle. This leader, Jesus, is a simple carpenter from the town of Nazareth, but He carries Himself with this great balance of courage and humility. He speaks with confidence and such depth, people begin to follow Him while religious leaders seek to destroy Him. Peter finds himself as one of the leaders of the followers of the ultimate leader, Jesus Christ of Nazareth. Throughout his life of leading and following, Peter experiences great highs and lows. He sees Jesus heal all sorts of maladies. He watches miracles of provision such as the first one he experienced with the miraculous catch. He sees Jesus feed multitudes of people with minimum resources. He sees this Man speak to the wind and waves to calm the seas. He even shares an unbelievable experience of walking on water before the fear of winds and waves sink him. Peter was a follower of a great leader (Jesus) and a leader of the first followers (disciples.) He learned leadership from the best. Toward the end of this Man's time on earth, Peter and some of the other followers experience an event that includes a humble act of service and profound teaching metaphor for leadership. At the end of Jesus' ministry on earth, he chose to wash the disciples' feet. Imagine walking in sandals or barefoot all day and entering a house to sit. Servants were often stationed near the entry with a wash basin to clean the leaders' feet. Jesus assumed this role as servant in the middle of his last meal with his closest followers, albeit, at the protest of his top lieutenant, Peter. Peter proclaimed that Jesus would never wash his dirty feet. Jesus' rebuke of Peter was something like, "If I don't wash your feet, you have no part in me and my work." Peter then requested a full body wash.

Leadership is not a popular term in the Bible. Jesus often had stinging rebukes for the religious leaders of his day, but he clearly demonstrated and defined leadership as servanthood. Jesus' method and message was one of power and love. In this life we lead, we can learn a lot from people who are simply trying to make ends meet, and suddenly they run into Someone who influences them to see so much more around them. Perhaps you are like Peter, cleaning your nets by the boat. Maybe you are finishing your last financial report, planning your next lesson, getting ready for your next big goal, or trying to discover your next steps. Throughout this book, I hope we can take this journey together with the expectation there may be that moment of "cleaning our nets" where we discover, when we least expect it, the extraordinary in the ordinary, supernatural in the natural, and provision in moments that don't always make sense. Common people living common lives can decide to dig deeper into principles that make this whole world go around. In the everyday tasks such as cleaning our nets and preparing our tools for the next job, we discover a new voice and find new provision for a new future. We can discover, like Peter, that we matter and we can learn to do things in new ways that impact people in new ways. People who matter can decide to do what matters and live a principle-centered life of purpose with great passion.

Many books on leadership, improvement strategy, personal self-help, devotional studies, and biographies already fill my bookshelf and perhaps yours as well. My desire in creating this work is to provide a new opportunity. I, like Peter, may be simply washing my nets by writing the principles and strategies I have toiled with in my years of teaching, learning, and leading. Perhaps while doing so, I discover, casting out these words and offering them as potential insights to others, there is a great harvest that could fill my net and cause me to discover a new way of fishing I never tried before. Perhaps this journey into leading people who matter to do things that matter will matter far more than either you or I know because there are seeds sown that grow exponentially when no one can see. Perhaps you and I will both discover a miracle in the mundane and share together discovery into ourselves the abundance of a catch that could only come by investing in principles and trusting we reap what we sow. If you are reading this book, you matter to me; and I hope the content will matter to you and lead you to do what matters. A summary of the aforementioned "what" is quickly discovered in the table of contents but the real discovery will appear when you obey the voice of your conscience, influenced by the Designer, and get busy doing the work of leading yourself on purpose so you can be fit to lead others. Let us begin.

I

C.P.R. – LEADERSHIP CHARACTER

PRINCIPLE INFLUENCES AND INFLUENCERS

> Do you not know that in a race all the runners run, but only one gets the prize? Run in such a way as to get the prize.
>
> — 1 CORINTHIANS 9:24 NIV

Growing up in a rural town in South Georgia afforded me exposure to many influences that shaped who I am today. The early years on the farm and on the cross-country courses have served to crystalize my views on leadership principles that matter with take-aways that I hope help us to do what matters. My life is not full of extraordinary stories, but there are events I can reflect on today and see a connection to lessons that, as I look back on, are worthy of taking note so they influence growth. I was born about a month and a half prior to my expected due date. I was only about four and a half pounds. Mom said that I spent most of my time for the first month and a half sleeping, except when I ate. Perhaps I wanted out of the womb before I was ready. I have typically lived life in a hurry. There were no real complications with this early arrival and life continued as usual.

Sometime around my sixth birthday, the first major event that shaped who I would become happened. A tumor slightly smaller than a golf ball was found in my left eye and had to be removed. The tumor was found to be benign; however, there were some tough experiences as a young child being poked and prodded and going through a scary surgery where your eye is removed so a tumor can be cut out. I experienced loss of vision for a short period of time when the tumor was removed. I was young enough that most of the memories are blurred, literally and figuratively, but a couple of stories that matter were birthed this time as well.

First, was the experiences of pain from a spinal tap. When I read about a spinal tap now, I don't know why my memories of pain and multiple needle pokes are so vivid. A spinal tap is described as a single needle in the lumbar region inserted to remove spinal fluid for testing. Technicians and doctors were testing me for leukemia and other possible ailments that I don't even recall. I felt like several nurses were holding me down on a table and sticking multiple needles in my back. I was a tough kid who rarely cried and demonstrated a high tolerance for pain, even for needles, as many were used during the testing and preparation for surgery. I don't know what it was about this spinal tap that hurt so badly and why those memories are still imprinted, inaccurate or not. I also have vivid "nightmare-like" memories of falling into depths of a black abyss with multi-color monkey bars all around. I was falling so fast that I was scared to reach out and touch the monkey bars for fear of breaking bones due to the speed of my descent. These stories taught me that the fear of what we are going through is often greater than the actual battles themselves. The spinal tap may have hurt, but it was temporary and nothing was discovered that altered my course for a normal life. The fear generated by this vision of falling and breaking bones on the multi-colored monkey bars was definitely an irrational fear that only exacerbated the uncomfortable memory. The surgery went off without a hitch, the tumor was removed and I received lots of cool presents like the Lone Ranger and Silver miniature action figures. I also got to eat lots of ice cream like Forrest Gump after being shot in the buttocks.

This story is special to me because it teaches me how God can use the challenges and struggles we face to build a faithful path of future obedience for His glory. Because of this experience and the recommendations of doctors to have my blood tested for markers (primarily leukemia) or other fears regarding this abnormal growth in my eye, my mom came to my room one night and gave me a mission. She taught me to visualize myself running in open fields and never getting winded or tired. She was intentionally teaching me to use the power of the mind to build a healthy vision for my future. Little did she know, I would one day choose to run competitively. The drive to run fast, train hard, and win earned me a scholarship to Berry College, where I would meet my wife and find my first career in leadership. The opening scripture referenced previously sums up the passion that began as a conversation on my single bed in Moultrie, Georgia. I would run for the prize. The prize I ultimately ran for was not the trophy or medal, but the execution of running well and finishing the course.

In my earlier years growing up, I played baseball and football and was excited to enter Spring Training at the end of my 8th grade year as a defensive back, punt returner, and wide receiver. I felt I had a real chance to get a scholarship as a two-sport star in baseball and football. This all changed when my parents brought me into their bedroom and sat me down to have a talk that would change my course significantly. I never felt good about those conversations that required the bedroom isolation. That usually included some correction with the rod (or leather belt.) Funny story about one such encounter. My sister and I once left the house and went somewhere without permission, and we earned the aforementioned corrective action of a spanking. Shannon, my elder sister by fourteen months, was not used to such correction as she made better choices than I consistently. I was ready for my punishment, but Shannon was crying uncontrollably prior to even receiving one stroke. I, being moved with compassion, offered to take her licks. Without even missing a beat (no pun intended), mom said, "Shut up boy, you ain't Jesus."

Anyway, this trip to the bedroom was not intended to be one where I got a beating or a spanking. This trip to the bedroom was for mom and dad to tell me that my dreams of playing football were over and that I was going to have to quit playing. I was devastated. I was taught to "honor your father and mother" so my reaction was subdued and mom and dad did not know the fury of my heart; however, I channeled all of that frustration into push ups, sit ups, and running. I remember that I was quite active and talkative in middle school, so my teacher asked mom if we had land where I could run and get out some energy before coming to his class. Perhaps this running thing was meant to be, and both my mom and my social studies teacher were prophetic. The year I was told that my football playing was over, I also happened to be in the science classroom of Ms. Patsy Aultman, the wife of Robert Aultman, who was the high school cross-country coach and distance coach for track. Coach Aultman invited me to start training with the cross-country team and I began running immediately.

I did not enjoy the running part a lot, but I enjoyed being in control of my outcomes. I wanted to win. The first race I ran was a 30K (18.6 mile) road race at St. Marks in Florida. I was supposed to run the first eleven miles and then get in the van and ride to the finish line, but that was not my style. I like to finish what I start. That race began a running career that landed me calls from some major schools in Georgia, including Georgia Tech. My dad is a University of Georgia graduate; and I thought I wanted to travel a similar path and run for the Bulldogs, but they never called. My junior year in high school was significant because we travelled from South Georgia to Berry College for a big invitational hosted in front of the majestic Ford Buildings, and I fell in love with the place. I placed well against some tough competition and started to get the attention of Dr. Robert Pearson, who was the cross-country coach and athletic director at Berry. I was totally floored that a cross-country coach would be the athletic director, but it was true. And Dr. Pearson offered me a scholarship to run for Berry College after I opened my senior campaign with a high finish at the Berry Invitational. The reason this ordering of my steps is so significant to me is because the experience at Berry prepared me for the best choice I ever made in leadership. I met my wife Amy at Berry and knew after our first date at Applebee's I was going to ask her to marry me. I did not know if she would say yes, and it was probably a good thing I waited because she did not know on our first date if she wanted to hang with me.

Four years of the toil of training and disciplining my body led to four years of scholarship compensation for competing at Berry College, where I would eventually learn many life lessons and cross paths with the key figure in the next phase of my life, my wife, Amy Louise Justice. The Bible gives us many examples of God's working in the lives of His servants where there is this intermingling of destiny, change, fate, and obedience outcomes. Not everything in my college days would reflect Godly character and obedient outcomes, but the beginning of a relationship that would create my most precious union on earth outside of my relationship with my Creator is not to be underplayed. What started as a conversation with my mom in my bedroom created a vision of running without growing weary that culminated into my steps being ordered into the next phase of my life. I discovered who I wanted to share my life with and what I wanted my life's work to be. As a result of my time running at Berry, I became a husband, a teacher, a father and servant. I learned at Berry that we must integrate hands (hard work), heart, (compassionate servanthood), and head (education and enlightenment through intentional study) in order to live a life of contribution that has the potential to create fulfillment for the individual and all those he/she influences.

The purpose of this first section of the book is to discover characteristics of leadership that help support and forge the The Heart of a Champion so one may run well to obtain the prize. Throughout my running career, there were many insights I learned. After I graduated from Berry, I swore I would never participate in distance running again. I embraced the oft quoted statement, "If I'm running, you better look around and see who's chasing me." I immediately began weightlifting and focused on getting stronger on the bench press. I would set one rep max targets and attack my weight training with tenacity and as I type this now, I am 230 pounds. I never reached my final bench press goal because I felt the stress on my shoulder would cause me to have problems the rest of my life if I didn't stop. I then took up High Intensity Interval Training and a variety of workout regimens that mimic those of the "Crossfit" world, minus the running. When my eldest son and my daughter both ventured into the world of cross-country in high school, I began running again to help Natalie with her training. The experience was much different. I ran much less competitive times and needed much more time to recover. At Berry, I ran two times daily, four days a week and one time two other days. Now I rarely run more than three times per week. When I ran in college, an eight-minute pace on the mile was a long slow distance day. Now that pace is intense for me. If someone had told me, at almost 50, I would be training a 230 pound body for a 50-mile ultra marathon, I would have laughed.

Running is a great metaphor for life. The apostle Paul would agree, hence the verses from 1 Corinthians chapter nine. Running was a way to laugh in the face of the fear that could have sidetracked my life during my early years. Remember mom's vision casting on my bed with the imagination and meditation of running without getting tired? Running became a way for me to connect with my wife and eventually my children. Running became a way to meet new friends and forge new relationships through the ultra running community. Most of all, running has finally become a way for me to discipline my body to train for a prize that is, most often, the satisfaction of trying to finish a race. I don't race to win a belt buckle or other form of trophy. I race to push myself and create opportunities for learning and growing. As we dive into the material related to the Heart of a Champion, consider the metaphor of an athlete, maybe even a runner, who disciplines his body for competition. The laws of nature are not free. You experience the best learning by inserting yourself into trials with the intent of pushing the body, mind, and spirit to get better.

> "Character cannot be developed in ease and quiet. Only through experiences of trial and suffering can the soul be strengthened, vision cleared, ambition inspired and success achieved."
>
> — HELEN KELLER

As we work to chisel away at the granite rock of life, sculpt the characteristics for excellence, and prepare to continuously put brush to canvas in the masterpiece of life, it is fitting that Helen Keller talks of trials and suffering that yields strength in the soul. When athletes strain and stress their bodies through trials and suffering, they find their bodies adapt and get stronger. Similarly, in life, when we put ourselves through the trials and suffering that has intended outcomes in specific mission orientations, the struggles make us stronger and more likely to eventually obtain the prize of a better life. If you are content with just making it or barely getting by, this writing is not for you. If you do not develop a passion for continuously improving or getting better, your reading of this work is a waste. If you have a heart that drives you passionately to pursue, with tenacity, things that often make people think you are overly motivated, or maybe even weird, you will probably understand where I stand. Challenges are inherent in competition. The history of competition as I understood it was often to prepare men and women for the battlefield of life.

As I played sports growing up, I often heard that this game or sport is a microcosm of life and lessons learned on the field or on the race course are transferable skills to this game of life. The ideas I am trying to communicate in The Heart of a Champion are simply ideas I hope are principle-centered roadmaps or lighthouses that help guide us on this journey as we avoid the harsh shores of shipwreck so, in the end we can say, I am a Champion. I often run races now and they are not races I expect to win in the sense of getting a first place medal or a wreath around my head. I do expect; however, to grow stronger leading up to the challenge and I want to feel like I've done well once the event is completed. I challenge my mind, body, and spirit to all integrate as one whole unified presence to help me get the most out of this journey, and there are some key guiding principles I think "shock the system" and reignite energy and life when this championship heart is weary, out of rhythm, or simply not beating. That is why I chose this acronym of C.P.R. C.P.R. contains three letters representing nine words that comprise an overarching framework for excellence in this championship lifestyle.

The three letters each have three words representing a connected message that reminds us of key attributes giving us access to powerful thoughts and language with which to develop an internal voice that speaks when it's time to be mission prepared and ready for each battle of life. I think it is so important for us to think about how we think and use our mind well. It is a wonderful tool and able to do so much more than anyone could truly know. Our Mindset, Mouth, and Motion are three important integrated parts leading to the accomplishment of our missions/goals. We have to think right, talk right, and act right if we want to live right. I hope the outlining of some key terms I believe impact our readiness will inspire you to continuously develop the tools of your mind and mouth so you develop The Heart of a Champion and inspire a healthy rhythm from which to live. Out of the abundance of the heart, your mouth speaks, and you have what you say. There is power in the spoken word by planting seeds in your heart and mind to cultivate your speech. Read these words and contemplate how they influence who you want to be: Courage, Commitment, Conqueror, Principles, Purpose, Passion, Respect, Responsibility, Right. These words will not create an exhaustive list of terms that build this character of leadership; however, they will provide a framework I believe will amplify the core characteristics for establishing a principle-centered approach to becoming a championship winner in everyday life.

2

THE HEART OF A CHAMPION: C.P.R.

Having spoiled the surprise, I will say that I love the number three. My favorite numbers are 3, 7, and 21. Three is unique to me because it represents the trinity. We are a triune being (spirit, soul and body) and our Creator is considered a Trinity as well (Father, Son, Holy Spirit.) Seven is the number of completion and 21 is the product of 3 and 7. My friends Chadd Wright and Blake Wright began a project/business called 3of7Project that incorporates this idea of becoming a complete human (7) through maintaining a healthy spirit, soul, and body (3) by challenging yourself to continuously feed and grow in all three domains.

It is this project that has inspired me to rewrite this version of C.P.R. as I process my leadership journey and share insights I have gained in my 47 years as a son (child), adult, husband, father, teacher, principal, church leader, friend, and CHAMPION! I've won some and lost some and continue to do so. I began sharing this concept of C.P.R. back in 2014 and will continue to learn and grow around these core attributes of effective self-leadership and/or self-mastery. May our journey through these words produce good insights and fruit as we strive to become the champions by LIVING LIFE LOUD. As we journey into the 3's of CPR, we will discover the connectedness of the

C's, the P's and the R's and their relationship to the overall health in this championship journey of life. Let's go!

3

THE THREE C'S: COURAGE, COMMITMENT, AND CONQUEROR

T he heart of the matter in The Heart of a Champion starts with the willingness to live with courage to demonstrate the consistent commitment to be a conqueror. As we dig into each word independently, keep in mind there is no such thing as a conclusive list of qualities or characteristics that complete us as humans. We are complex beings with a multiplicity of facets from which to improve our living posture, but I believe the three C's are a great starting point to jumpstart our heart just like the pulse from an AED. If your heart lacks passion or is out of rhythm, check the three C's.

COURAGE

Winston Churchill said courage is the preeminent virtue because it guarantees all the others. What is courage? Many mistake bravery with courage. A person may be brave when the actual virtue of courage is absent. Dr. Mark Rutland wrote a book I love called *Hanging by a Thread*. In his writing about courage, he articulated the little child that wants to swing higher may be brave or even reckless and we might describe that person as courageous. The kamikaze pilots of Japan were considered to have courage. Perhaps they were just scared young men motivated by a perverted sense of duty and a dangerous level of alcohol.

Warriors of old have summoned up the courage to do great feats in battle that, in my estimation may have resembled crazy more than courage. Courage is not the absence of fear and thus may require fear to be in operation. When we dull the sense of fear with some outside chemical, are we courageous? I don't know for sure, but the greatest examples of courage to me are the people who struggle through life with some difficult challenge and find the strength to continuously overcome disability or challenge through will power and grit. In his [1]book, *Hanging By a Thread,* author Mark Rutland writes, "The distinction between a hero and an obnoxious show-off is defined by character." In the absence of character, there is no courage. Courage, according to Merriam-Webster online dictionary, is "mental or moral strength to venture, persevere, and withstand danger, fear, or difficulty." Courage starts in the mind and is summoned when strength is needed to persevere in a difficult or dangerous situation. When life's challenges get hard and you summon the strength of character to press on one step at a time and not quit, the fuel to that fire is most definitely courage.

Amy and I were challenged with the decision to take a pay cut and keep her home to invest in our children or to have her continue teaching and make it easier to have more material things. I believe courage to do what we felt was right won out over the fear of us and our kids not having all the same levels of comfort others around us enjoy. We accrued some painful debt as a result of this choice and a poorly managed budget; however, we had the courage to prioritize our family in the way we felt we were called to do while being responsible to pay all we owed. I am not making a judgement and saying all families should operate that way, but courage requires that you follow your beliefs from your heart and make choices consistent with them. Courage may manifest itself in the simple decisions to summon up strength to persevere in adverse situations you create. Courage may also manifest itself in situations you did not create but could not avoid. I have a third sister as a result of a drunk driver killing her parents. My parents made the courageous decision to adopt Tammy as they felt they were in the best position to provide a positive future life for "Tambo" (my affectionate nickname for her.) Tammy faces challenges from a traumatic brain injury that make some life events unlikely such as driving a car, getting married, living independently, etc. In conversation with her, I discovered she's not missing out in life. I asked her what was going well for her and what she wished was different. She told me she is thankful for her family. She is always positive and happy to be living. She couldn't come up with anything she wanted to be different. Courage enables all other virtues because it allows you to summon the energy to do what is right in moments when there is a great personal cost, fear, or challenge that is guaranteed to bring adversity.

 "Courage is the willingness to deny my own flesh and do what is noble, regardless of the cost."

— DR. MARK RUTLAND

Chadd Wright (U.S. Navy SEAL, retired) talks about challenges in his life and often refers to them as the "furnace of adversity." When the heat is turned up, how will you respond? Chadd faced the heat when he was disqualified from pursuing his dream of becoming a Navy SEAL due to a rare pericardial cyst on his heart. This cyst was not a problem for ordinary living, but could become problematic (even life-threatening) for Naval Special Warfare's required diving tasks. Chadd could have just stopped trying and accepted the disqualification by finding another path, but he summoned the courage to find a doctor willing to do the surgery. After getting himself back into shape after recovery, he stood in front of the same dive medical officer to be cleared for his chance on the start line to continue the pursuit of his dream. After twelve years of faithful service in one of the world's most elite special forces, he now shares that story and other great stories of courage in the face of adversity he has experienced. The secret sauce in any fantastic story of overcoming this furnace of adversity, is courage.

Note: Chadd Wright's story is worth pursuing. There are plenty of podcasts available as well as his own website: 3of7project.com where you learn more from him, his brother Blake Wright and other men and women about principles of completing yourself SPIRIT, SOUL, and BODY.

Courage is the preeminent virtue and provides within man's character the backdrop for the execution of all other fruits of good character. Courage may be found in the simple acts of doing the right thing such as returning the dropped twenty-dollar bill and returning it to the person you saw drop it. It may fuel taking a stand and speaking the truth in a situation that causes you discomfort or pain. It may be the leap taken by the Secret Service Agent to protect the President. Courage in any instant is the "character Super Glue" that sticks you to the right action in the face of danger, fear, or difficulty. The Heart of a Champion fortifies the individual with courage so the other characteristics of greatness can operate seamlessly. A call to courage comes regularly as we face life that always promises to bring challenges whose characteristics will surely wilt the faint at heart, the coward. Be strong and courageous because that is what is required in The Heart of a Champion.

COMMITMENT

The second "C" is commitment. Sometimes commitment is tested and your best energy is given to hanging on until you see another end that is more agreeable. In sharing Chadd's story, I think it goes without saying he was committed to becoming a Navy SEAL. The etymology of the word commitment is in understanding its roots. It comes from Latin *committere* which means "to join together, engage, place in the keeping of, entrust, bring about, carry out (a crime.)" Commitment requires integrity of heart to join your intent, actions and trust in such a way that you carry out or finish something. Consider the old saying, "When the going gets tough, the tough get going." I think the commitment or constant engagement of oneself in a worthy venture is a good way to define commitment. The antithesis of commitment is quitting. Commit to what you can finish. It's so common today to find people who are great starters and poor finishers. "I'm no longer going to commit because that's not what I meant." Courage and commitment go hand in hand as voiced in this quote by Winston Churchill, "Success is not final, failure is not fatal: it is the courage to continue that counts." That is commitment. In the face of failures and/or successes, commitment drives us to completion and to the starting line of the next challenge. Commitment is a choice.

> "When you reach the end of your rope, tie a knot in it and hang on."
>
> — GEORGE WASHINGTON

I remember my first attempt at an ultra marathon running with my friends Chadd and Blake Wright at Duncan Ridge Trail. I was faltering and not able to keep the pace I knew we needed to make the turn around and I truly felt like quitting and returning to the last aid station. I asked for Blake's phone to call my wife, Amy, so she could wait there for me. When we stopped for Blake to reach into his pack for his phone, Chadd looked me in the eyes and said, "Are you sure you want to do this?" I still remember that moment very vividly because the choice I made defined the failure. If I would have quit, I would not have given my total commitment to the mission. I continued the mission and encouraged them to go on ahead of me. This allowed me to get to the aid station at the "half-way" point of this race. There was a cutoff that I missed by 6 minutes; however, I did not quit. I truly left it all on the trail and remained true to my commitment to do all I could to finish. It was still a failure, but I can say that the failure felt much different than it would have for me to return to the truck back down the hill taking the easy way. You choose where you give your energy and you count on committed people. They are not easily swayed by challenge, danger, and pain. Committed people face challenges with vigor and a desire to finish well. I considered quitting due to the strain I felt I was placing on Chadd and Blake by holding them up in the race, but I felt a bigger responsibility of working to learn and grow without wearing the label of quitter. There is no shame in giving in to injury or stopping something because wisdom dictates such a decision, but commitment is clear where integrity is sound.

Commitment in our society is often short-lived. Over 50% of all marriage commitments end in divorce. Athletes commit and decommit based on the benefit their commitment is to them rather than to the institution. Students commit to college and get a degree. When they enter the workforce, they make another commitment, garner skills and quickly look to change commitments again when they think the grass is greener somewhere else. I'm not saying there aren't de-commitments that are advisable and healthy; however, there is a real trend in our failure to take responsibility for our choices and allow opportunities for growth through the natural processes of challenge and relationship. May we have the heart of a champion and always practice the making and keeping of commitments to ourselves, to our families, and to those who do so with us. Commitment is a key attribute that allows one to stay in the refining fire and forge the grit to endure hardship and come out a fine piece worthy of honor.

CONQUEROR

 "For a man to conquer himself is the first and noblest of all victories."

— PLATO

Just like leadership starts with self, so does conquering. I believe this word is another word for overcomer. It is not meant to promote warlords who conquer territories for control of more earth and people. I believe we are designed to conquer in life. We are to conquer fear, conquer missions worthy of our efforts, and conquer the domains of our existence where we are called to rule. Good conquerors love and appreciate the land and inhabitants of their conquest. In this acronym, we have discussed the powerful virtue of courage and the sticking power of commitment. The end goal is conquering and taking of the ground you are designed to take as the conqueror. The etymology of the words based in Latin tell us more about my thoughts behind the appropriate use of this word. The prefix "con" means "to search for, procure by effort, win" and the root in the middle of the word is "query" which means "to seek or gain." The word question starts with "query" and it means to seek the answer. The word conqueror being a noun is defined by me based on this etymology as a person who is in

18

search of or seeking the procurement of a win through effort. We are to be conquerors because The Heart of a Champion seeks to courageously pursue challenges and obstacles in life with a commitment to win. We want to win at marriage, win at raising children, win at our jobs (raises and promotions), win in friendships, win in our health, win in our recreation, win in our faith, and win in our stewardship for all we are responsible for. We are conquerors because we want to seek out a win in what matters to us.

Dale Carnegie is the author of several good books and the developer of self-improvement material still used today to impact businesses/organizations and individuals. He [2]said, "Don't be afraid to give your best to what seemingly are small jobs. Every time you conquer one it makes you that much stronger. If you do the little jobs well, the big ones will tend to take care of themselves." Being faithful in the little things means as you conquer the smaller manageable challenges of daily life, organically the strength gained from these conquests deliver on bigger scales (law of the harvest.)

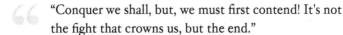 "Conquer we shall, but, we must first contend! It's not the fight that crowns us, but the end."

— ROBERT HERRICK

We must figure out which parts of our lives represent rings worthy of our entry to contend. We must fight the good fight and expect to win. We must know all fights eventually do come to an end. The conqueror is one who has the courage to toe the line, the commitment to prepare for the battle and subject his body to the challenges and stressors that will make him stronger for the fray, and the mentality so victory at the end happens before the entry into the arena. Prepare now for your championship life by developing courage, commitment, and the mentality of a conqueror as you prepare for the next steps in the journey.

4

THE THREE P'S: PRINCIPLES, PURPOSE, AND PASSION

R ight in the center of the acronym for CPR is the heart of the matter, the 3 P's. Principles lead, purpose drives, and passion fuels. Simon Sinek wrote a bestselling book entitled *Start with Why: How Great Leaders Inspire Everyone to Take Action*. His TED Talk on the subject was an inspiring look into purpose and the importance of authentically identifying your why so the depths of your work are supported with a passion that is sustainable. These 3 P's serve a unique purpose as a potential anchor that assists us with really identifying our personal vision, mission, and values. Stephen Covey in his 1989 timeless classic, *The 7 Habits of Highly Effective People,* teaches the second habit of "begin with the end in mind." His articulation of this habit includes the explanation of desired outcomes and how the ultimate desired outcome is the desired outcome of our lives. What do you want people to say about your "dash?" My father in-law, Henry Grady Justice, passed away and was blessed to have thousands of people attend his visitation and funeral. He never earned a college degree, but he lived in such a way that garnered a reputation of being everyone's best friend. He brought energy and joy with him and he finished what he started. Reading my wife's eulogy that she so eloquently delivered at the funeral was confirmation that the work we do now to prepare for that day is worth it because it celebrates life well lived while giving hope to the ones still toiling. I want to produce fruit that is evidence of a principle-centered approach to life with a clear and evident "why" that fuels my passion for excellence.

PRINCIPLES

The 3 P's of a champion starts with principles. Imagine, if you will, Sir Isaac Newton, going on a hike as he contemplates the forces of nature when a sudden breeze blows and an apple falls from a tree. The consistent replication of cycles such as this, cause people like Newton, Albert Einstein and many other great scientists to study and develop theories about natural laws or principles that govern our universe. There are principles or natural laws all around us that serve as lighthouses in the distance to help navigate the ship of our life away from the shoreline. Principles govern. We think we have control. We only control ourselves. Everything else is governed by principles. Like gravity, our opinion does not matter; however, our understanding of gravity's operation and its impact on the real world can help us learn to make choices that respond appropriately to things that we can't control. Gravity does not get emotional nor does it change its operation based on the people in its presence. Gravity consistently works to bring order and predictability to our universe so we can use other natural laws to overcome its effects (like the law of lift in physics.) Principles are natural laws that are self-evident and real. We do not see the world as it is, but we see it as we are. We interpret reality based on our knowledge and understanding. This vision in our perspective of "how things are" is called a paradigm. We can't change principles, but we can change or adjust our paradigm. The Bible says that "...as he thinketh in his heart, so is he." We are a product of our thoughts. That is why it is so important to renew our minds (see Romans 12:1-2 KJV.)

Principle-centered people tend to be more at peace with themselves and those around them because they are making decisions based on a paradigm that is aligned to principles that are unchanging. It is worth time invested in seeking out principles, or natural laws, so our life choices are principle informed. For instance, consider the greatest law of the Kingdom articulated by Jesus of Nazareth. In one of Jesus' parables, we are taught a seed goes into the ground and dies but later reproduces more life after its own kind (law of harvest.) From Genesis to Revelation, we see this Kingdom principle play out and we see it in our own lives. Paul tells the Galatians 6:7, "Be not deceived; God is not mocked, for whatsoever a man soweth, that shall he also reap." We do well to recognize natural laws such as this one and consider them in our everyday life. In my years as an educator, I have consistently admonished students to "treat others the way you want to be treated." We often say, "what goes around comes around." We know this truth to be evident and yet, if we fail to consider principles, we miss the opportunity to plant good seeds.

Champions see truth in nature and work to apply truth both metaphorically and practically in life's decisions, choices, and/or actions. Take some time to step away from reading this paragraph and consider the principles or natural laws you can observe in nature. Consider the principles or rules you were taught for living and evaluate whether or not they align with reality. Martin Luther King, Jr. and other civil rights activists used a principle articulated by our Declaration of Independence and referenced by Abraham Lincoln to undergird the dream, "We hold these truths to be self-evident...that all men are created equal and are endued by their Creator with certain inalienable rights..." Some may say that rules are made to be broken, but the rules that are set forth by the Creator are not. Where principles lead, good success follows. We were designed to operate with certain specifications that are governed by principles. Just as the athlete learns specificity for training to help improve performance, pilots learn about laws of lift to fly, sailors learn about buoyancy and tides to succeed in the ocean, we must learn about the laws that govern our A.O. (area of operation) and discipline ourselves to harmonize or walk in integrity with them.

PURPOSE

The principles of purpose come next. I believe it is critical for a person to identify natural laws and principles that govern because we are made to govern and have dominion in a way that promotes positive growth and change. Purpose driven people set clearly targeted goals and objectives that align to overall mission and beliefs. Purpose is our WHY! Start with the WHY, remember the WHY, clarify the WHY, and finish the WHY! WHY clarifies purpose and motivates passionate pursuit toward an end (vision) that is worthy of the energy applied. It is my belief that purpose is clearly defined in the beginning. Let us consider Genesis 1:28 in the King James Version of the Bible: "And God blessed them, and God said unto them, Be fruitful, and multiply, and replenish the earth, and subdue it: and have dominion over the fish of the sea, and over the fowl of the air, and over every living thing that moveth upon the earth." According to the beginning in the ancient texts, Adam was created by God forming him in the dust of the earth and breathing "ruwah" into him, making him a living soul. The detailed description of creation reveals to us some natural laws of design that are significant. Everything God made prior to Adam was spoken into existence and the phrase used was "let there be;" however, when the Designer made Adam the phrase was "Let us (Father, Son, and Holy Spirit) make man in our image and our likeness." Everything was made after its own kind. God made Adam in his image and told him to be fruitful, multiply, replenish, and subdue. These words indicate man's purpose.

I believe the fruitful, multiply, replenish, and subdue along with "let him have dominion" was referring to all that God had made with the phrase "let there be." Man was not; however, given dominion over man. It is my humble opinion that one of the most powerful expressions of leadership is submission. Man was told to have dominion over birds, fish, and cattle, but he was not given dominion over the man created in God's image. Leadership is not dominion. Leadership is servanthood. Adam was to rule over creation that had the designation of "let there be" because it was all created to serve as a place God could set up colonies where He is the King of kings, but we are the king or ruler of our domain or our area leadership. Consider the Lord's Prayer. "Our Father who art in heaven, hallowed be thy name. Thy kingdom come, thy will be done, in earth as it is in heaven." Dr. Mark Rutland articulated that he believes this "in earth" may actually mean in the earthen vessel of our lives. Our purpose is to reproduce the Kingdom fruit from our Heavenly Father and bring heavenly purposes to earth through the relationship we have with the King. We are ambassadors on this earth with the purpose of enjoying this beautiful creation, taking care of it, and facilitating its fruitfulness while multiplying in ours.

Purpose is baked into our DNA by our Designer and we all have an innate desire for leadership and dominion. Good leaders are resourceful, respectful to the resources they have access, and supremely respectful of the highest order of creation that is man made in His image and likeness. What do we take away from this focus on the origin of man and the discovery of purpose? We should take away a realization that we have great responsibility to consider these principles and find our niche or lane. We have to discover our WHY and apply our gifts, talents, and energy to it. Choices are better aligned when there is an end or purpose for which they are intentionally made. That ultimate purpose is our personal mission, family mission, and professional mission. I have spent significant time and energy in creating my personal, family, and professional mission statements so I am able to put into words a life on purpose. Lead people who matter to do things that matter is that personal mission statement that drives and undergirds all that I do as a person. When you spend time considering what your life is, the principles you embrace as priority, along with intentional actions, you will create your best life by not merely letting life happen.

Stephen Covey articulates these in the three choices that lead to everyday greatness. These are the choice to act, the choice of purpose, and the choice for principles. The choice to act is when we decide that our choices matter and we are a product of them rather than the circumstances that surround us. The choice of purpose is to begin with the end or desired outcome in mind where we act on the responsibility of the first choice and plan for the desired results. The third choice is the choice for principles where we prioritize choices based on desired outcomes of our design rather than just accepting current reality as eternal. We cannot just throw our hands up and say, "It is what it is." We may have to live with some realities of circumstances surrounding us, but we must tap into our purpose to change what we should and to impact our surroundings. The good in us is there for a reason and without discovering our purpose, we miss the reason for which we were created. Live on purpose.

PASSION

Purpose is often articulated in vision and mission, but purpose has to be executed. Passion is the energy to execute around your principled purpose. It's interesting how interconnected these three characteristics of leadership are. Oftentimes a person's purpose creates a passion for execution, but perhaps just as often, a person's experiences motivate passion which creates new vision and purpose. Passion is a root of compassion. Compassion moved Christ. Love with a mission is compassion. Passion is one's drive to do something or get something done. We have to engage our lives in meaningful pursuits that drive us. This drive in us is called passion. Michael Jr., the comedian, clarified with a man in his audience the connection between purpose and passion. He asked the man what he did. The man said he was a mechanic. The man said he fixes people's cars all day long. Eventually Michael Jr. established that the man's real purpose was to help people to arrive at their destination. That passion is much more relevant when we see what we are doing as a kingdom purpose and/or mandate. It is interesting that the finished work of Christ on the cross is called the Passion. I think it most appropriate that passion follows purpose and that purpose follows principles. Let's be passionate pursuers of purpose by using principles as a compass to guide and direct our works in a meaningful direction.

The 3 P's are the heart of CPR because there is the potential for everything that should motivate us to live well to be sharpened in the pursuit of each of them. Consider the reality that at the outset of every start up, leadership teams consider vision, mission, and beliefs. These three components are embedded in the 3 P's. Take some time to consider what principles should guide your everyday life (beliefs.) What are the principles by which you will be governed? Discover your WHY or your desired outcomes that really speak to the purpose (mission and vision) of your life or organization. What are you a producer of and what should be the outcome of your efforts or your organization? Lastly, what drives your economic engine? What drives you to excel? What do you really want to be good at or known for? What is your passion (vision, mission, and belief)? In a good mission statement, the 3 three P's are addressed in some manner. Consider my mission statement: Lead people who matter to do things that matter. Can you infer the statement principles (people matter, execution matters), purpose (connection of leading and doing what matters), and passion (implication of matter)? Invest in your own design to create your personal vision, mission, and beliefs so you are able to live a principle-centered life, on purpose, passionately.

5

THE THREE R'S: RESPECT, RESPONSIBILITY, RIGHT

The 3 R's of leadership character are respect, responsibility and right. The 3 C's are the catalysts or motivating characteristics for leadership growth and change. Courage undergirds commitment and together these first two C's prepare for the mindset of a conqueror. The 3 P's represent the heart or core of these virtues. These P's of principle, purpose, and passion provide an anchor of stability that connects us to a life of purpose. The 3 R's are where the rubber meets the road. The 3 P's help us with the WHY and the 3 R's really get into the HOW. If we work on identifying and aligning the core principles, as well as clarifying our purpose and passion, we must use the 3 R's to carry out our mission.

RESPECT

Respect is a word often overcomplicated and understated. Respect comes from a very clear root word of value. We tend to respect what we value. As an educational leader, one of the first things I do each year is hold assemblies by grade level where I speak to students about the 3 R's. During this talk, I attempt to clearly articulate for the kids what respect is. Consider a cell phone and a tennis ball. Imagine me holding a cell phone in my hand and pretending I am going to throw it to

Coach Rogers in the back of the room. I wind up and step toward my target and deliver a pretend pristine throwing motion, yet I decide to hold on to the expensive cellular device. Meanwhile, the kids are all getting wide eyed and thinking about whether or not Coach Rogers can catch. They process, in their own way, whether they feel I held off on the throw because I didn't trust Coach Rogers. They may entertain other thoughts or judgments based on their own background knowledge and observations. I typically laugh at their response and gasp of relief when they recognize I have not thrown the iPhone. Almost immediately, I take the tennis ball and throw it to Coach Rogers and he catches it. What is your "take away" from imagining this presentation? Students are easily able to explain to me that they think I chose not to throw the phone because it costs a lot of money and Coach Rogers may not catch it. I continue asking questions until I get them to two major understandings. First, the phone is valuable and costs too much money for me to throw like a tennis ball. Second, the phone was not designed to be thrown like a ball. Its purpose is to do a lot of things, but none of those things involve throwing and catching. The tennis ball was within its purpose; however, the phone would not have been. We would say that using a phone as a ball is abnormal, right?

Abnormal use is often dangerously close to abuse. When we respect something, we value its purpose and usefulness. I like to teach that we respect ourselves, others, and things (or the environment.) Respecting yourself means that you identify your purpose or usefulness and value the potential contributions within your sphere of influence. I love that the book of Matthew summarizes in Christ's words the whole law in two commands. The first was that we are to love God with all our heart, soul, mind and strength and the second was to love our neighbor as ourselves. In the second part of this command there are actually two parts; we cannot love our neighbors until we love ourselves. This truth carries over to this idea of respect yourself (first), respect others, and respect things. I often hear "You gotta give respect to get respect." I believe that such a statement is consistent with the law of the harvest; however, when you are talking about one's control over choices, you can still give respect regardless of what others choose. Respecting ourselves or seeing our own value really comes into clear sight through the work of discovering the 3 P's and doing the work of owning ours. We must begin with valuing the unique gifts and talents that are given to us as individuals. We, as individuals, are extremely gifted and special; however, we are not any more special than the next person. We simply have more ability to control the value we add to life by our choices. We are in control of our attitudes and we determine how we ascribe value and to whom. We must recognize and appreciate the enormous potential in ourselves. Once we see through the lens of greatness in terms of potential, it is much easier to appreciate others and exhibit respect and tolerance toward them. We are all different and have uniqueness that distinguishes us. We should appreciate and value people. We all bleed red blood regardless of skin color, religious beliefs, and/or gender.

One of the greatest commands we find in the New Testament is to not show "respect of persons" based on their wealth and prestige. God himself is "no respecter of persons," but He demonstrated His value in that He gave his only Son as a sacrifice for our sins so we would not be condemned but saved. If He values people that much, while they are still "sinners," we should take notice and make sure we value and respect people. Resources and "things" are here to serve creation. The books of Proverbs and Genesis teach us to respect animals and to take care of or tend to the earth around us. Adam's first directive was to tend the garden and it would take care of him. We often speak of abuse. The simple definition of abuse is "abnormal use." When we use a thing for something other than its intended purpose we diminish its effectiveness and run the risk of damaging or even destroying. Environmentalism in balance engenders the first two R's of respect and responsibility. The same thing is true of people. When people are abused, they are not as likely to realize their full potential and can run the risk of being trapped into purposeless, aimless living. Respect is a cornerstone paradigm that provides a foundation for the other R's. In the words of Benjamin Disraeli, "The greatest good we can do for another is not to share your riches but to reveal to him his own."

RESPONSIBILITY

 "Few men are lacking in capacity, but they fail because they are lacking in application."

— CALVIN COOLIDGE

Many people claim to want to be "responsible," but few really want to pay the price. We are all "RESPONSE – ABLE" but we are not all responding based on our abilities and gifts. President Coolidge said it well. Steady application and consistent responding to the capacity within us is responsibility. Most of our world's problems are a problem of responsibility. Insurance companies fight over who is responsible for the bills. Small claims courts consistently deal with someone's responsibility or irresponsibility. Taking responsibility for one's attitudes and actions induces effective behavior. The first habit that Stephen Covey brings out is "be proactive." That habit says that, between stimulus and response, there is a space and in this space rests our POWER to choose. What will you choose? Will you choose to discipline yourself to be teachable and to be a person who consistently increases his/her capacity to improve? Responsible people manage themselves well and avoid focusing too much energy on the stimuli that cannot be controlled or changed. Nelson Rockefeller said, "I believe that every right implies a responsibility; every opportunity, an obligation, every possession, a duty." Responsibility is the duty we each have to ourselves and others to integrate our obligations and resources in ways that contribute appropriately to self and society.

You can't control the weather, but you can get an umbrella. Stephen Covey would say, "Make your own weather." Accepting responsibility empowers us to be in the driver's seat and promotes in us the willingness to stretch ourselves and our abilities. This responsible behavior begins in the mind. James Allen said, "Good thoughts bear good fruit, bad thoughts bear bad fruit-and man is his own gardener." Our minds are the battlefield of life. Expectations and circumstances tend to be mixed in the gymnasium of our mind and we decide how we will respond. When our expectations are not met and the circumstances we face are not to our liking, we tend to seek a scapegoat in the form of a person, place or thing to relieve us of blame. Our will is a powerful tool, but the work of aligning our purpose and passion with principles requires the courageous commitment to conquer the "scapegoat" mentality and the blame game.

The champion's mindset is to take responsibility for current reality by moving toward nurturing thoughts that yield fruitful action. Jocko Willink and Leif Babin in their [1]book *Extreme Ownership* articulate "the most fundamental and important truth at the heart of Extreme Ownership: there are no bad teams, only bad leaders." In the book, Jocko tells a story of a boat crew that is always finishing last. The instructors take the leader from the winning boat crew and place him in the losing boat crew and eventually that losing boat crew begins to win. I believe one fundamental concept seen throughout any discussion on improvement, self or organizational, says leadership starts with me. The observations I make in my family, my organization, and anywhere I believe I have influence are a testimony of my leadership and they tell me my level of effectiveness. Responsible people build responsible teams who build responsiveness into the organization. The essence of responsible leadership is responsible execution of the key steps or strategies that bring desired results. When circumstances and challenges mount, will you take the responsibility to right the ship or will you just blame the wind and the waves? Responsible people assess where they are continually and work to make sure they don't stay in one place.

Objects at rest tend to stay in rest. Champions move and conquer. How are you maximizing the endowments and opportunities before you to create momentum toward the movement in producing the right desired outcomes in your daily life? Every moment of life offers you moment by moment opportunities to respond. Uncle Ben, Spiderman's uncle said, "With great power comes great responsibility." You have the never ending power to choose. To what end will my choices lead? That's a good question to ask consistently. Those choices lead to a result. Responsible people embrace this truth and stand firm on the decision to use their abilities for what is right.

RIGHT

Consider a plumb line. These weights on a string are now replaced by lasers. The laser or plum line are basically both a point of reference to identify what is "plumb" or square. I am one of those who notices the picture in the room that is crooked. I remember, when I finished my room in the basement and I was putting up the frame for the acoustic ceiling, I had a friend in the contracting business who offered his laser to help me make straight lines on the wall without having to mark them. That laser was attached to the starting grid and a red light went around the room repeatedly and so I could attach the first rail and set all the middle supports in the framework of that ceiling. If that laser hit the rail, instead of the wall, I knew I had to raise the railing. In our life, there is a plumb line or a laser transit that we have inside of us called our conscience. Often referred to as a "still small voice," Mr. Jiminy Cricket, from Disney's *Pinocchio*, would always admonish us to let this voice be our guide. On the highway, we have those indentations in the road on the outside of the white line that you hear when you veer over because you are looking at your phone or radio. That annoying sound may save a life or a car part or two as that annoying road lets you know that you are not on the right (correct) side of the line. Standing on the side of the right is important for us as leaders and champions. We need to invest in searching for principles that lead or serve as our guide so we have a point of reference like that rope with a weight at the bottom or that laser light that lets me know if I am laying out the track right.

When I first thought of the final "R" to use for this character trait, I considered using righteous or righteousness, but I was concerned there would be confusion around aligning yourself with good choices vs. what you cannot earn. Righteousness is an inheritance that is hard to accept and receive because it is such an amazing gift. We are the righteousness of God in Christ if we are Christ's. I think it is important to distinguish between the right choices that are fruits from your life vs. the grace afforded to be right because of what Christ did on the cross. I believe that C.P.R. represents leadership character that we can directly influence by our choices. We cannot be righteous because of our choices, but we can make choices to stand on the side of right. I am the righteousness of God in Christ Jesus and, as a result, I really desire that my fruit align with what is right. We cannot earn this; however, we have been given the opportunity to be this. We all desire to be right and on the side of right. Imagine the purity of conscience when we are able to avoid the condemnation that comes with disobedience and be able to look into the mirror of our heart and see Jesus. We have this treasure in earthen vessels. We have the treasure of His Law written, not on tablets of stone, but on the tablets of our heart. Champions are real with themselves, they evaluate their level of performance and set a path to train and overcome what is not RIGHT in their lives so they can strive for mastery. Paul said in I Corinthians that he keeps his body under subjection so he can obtain a prize.

> *"Know ye not that they which run in a race run all, but one receiveth the prize? So run, that ye may obtain. And every man that striveth for the mastery is temperate in all things. Now they do it to obtain a corruptible crown; but we an incorruptible. I therefore so run, not as uncertainly; so fight I, not as one that beateth the air: But I keep under my body, and bring it into subjection: lest that by any means, when I have preached to others, I myself should be a castaway."*

— I CORINTHIANS 9:24-27 KJV

Championship living requires discipline, pain ("no pain, no gain"), rest, and challenge. Will you challenge yourself to be better or will you just accept where you are? To truly integrate this character trait of a champion, one must think right, talk right, and live right. We know what is right by the principles we learn from great leaders and mentors in our lives. Continuous improvement requires that we grow in the knowledge of what is good and right and that we work on our decision making and take responsibility for them. To think right, we must carefully choose what we take in through our eyes and ears. Our thoughts become our actions. If you think right, you will talk right.

Proverbs 23:7 tells us "For as he thinketh in his heart, so is he." Guard your heart and mind. Be intentional with your reading, watching, and listening. Eventually what is in your heart because of your thinking will come out of your mouth. Our mouth speaks from what is in our heart and Proverbs chapter 4 teaches us to watch over our heart with diligence. The spoken word is powerful. Later in this work we will delve into the power of our words, but suffice it to say, that we have what we say according to Mark 11:23. Thinking right and talking right will lead to doing right. Our actions follow our will. We get to choose and we feed the choice mechanism by transforming our thoughts to align with what agrees with His truth (Romans 12:1-2.) His Word is the plumb line. Thinking right leads to talking right. Talking right leads to walking right. Walking right leads to being right. In the heart of a champion is this opportunity to align right thinking, talking, and walking with the righteousness of the work Christ wrought in you by His obedience to death on a cross. Will you take advantage of this choice you have to be right with God and demonstrate appreciation by obedience? It's always right to love and treat others the way you want to be treated. It's always right to humble yourself and put others first. It's always right to be honest and truthful in all of your dealings. It's always right to pay what you owe. It's always right to forgive others and walk in peace.

Will you take the challenge or just wait until you are rushed until you are thrown off balance? It's time for a life of C.P.R. Champions, rise up and be who you are called to be. Champions courageously demonstrate commitment to be a conqueror. There is no quit in a champion. Principle-centered leaders pursue purpose with passion and passionately pursue their purpose. The reciprocal operations of the three P's are a powerful reality. Passion and purpose are inspiring and effective in energy production when governed by principles. The three R's round out a champion's leadership qualities. A champion respects himself, others, and things. This respect prompts responsibility around the desire to live right and be right with our Creator. Whether or not we ever realize it, we are made to be living epistles written by the finger of God. We should demonstrate in our lives "good works." Faith without works is dead. Be a champion by keeping your heart with all diligence. Out of the heart, the whole life flows. In conclusion, be strong and courageous with a commitment to finish what you start and to become a conqueror in your life. Align yourself with principle-centered values so you live purposefully with a passion to execute your life's mission. Respect yourself, others, and things so you can be responsible stewards of your time, talent, and energy as you take a stand to live right.

II

LIVE LIFE LOUD

I envision C.P.R serving as a basic ethos or the characteristic spirit of a leader. If C.P.R. is the foundational character of the leader, LIVE LIFE LOUD is an extensive acronym for the "walking it out." It is easy to talk about good characteristics and what we hope to see, but to live it out is the real test of effectiveness. Can we ask ourselves, does living out of this framework have the effect in ways that can be counted on for similar replication in the future? Principle-centered leadership with the underpinnings of C.P.R. at its core is followed with LIVE LIFE LOUD as the "battle cry" of a life of meaning. The purpose of an acronym that is easy to remember in both C.P.R. and LIVE LIFE LOUD is to create easy neuropathways that make connections to principles easy to recall and accessible so we can think about them consistently.

As we think intentionally about how we live our life, our actions will follow that intent. It is time for us to discover the power of living with intentional focus. Many previous writings on leadership yield plenty of ways to think about leadership and many of the principles in this section will repeat or be congruent with much of what has already been said. LIVE LIFE LOUD, in my hope, is a statement of command that will teach, remind, inspire, and influence us to integrate with a clear vision the actions necessary for us to lead ourselves and others well as we demonstrate love for our Designer and all that He has designed. Leadership, as influence, starts with your influencing yourself to LIVE LIFE LOUD!

6

LEAD WITH INTEGRITY AROUND A VISION FOR EXCELLENCE!

"Leadership is becoming yourself so that you may benefit others."

— DR. MYLES MUNROE

Leadership is a popular term, yet it is so over-talked and under-achieved. We must first lead ourselves before we can lead others. It is critical that we find the truths in principles that are timeless and self-evident so we can build a life on a foundation that will not crumble. The first person you must lead is you. Mahatma Gandhi said a lot, but below are two impactful quotes I have enjoyed learning from:

The only tyrant I accept in this world is the "still small voice" within me. We mirror the world. All the tendencies present in the outer world are to be found in the world of our body. If we could change ourselves, the tendencies in the world would also change. As a man changes his own nature, so does the attitude of the world change towards him. This is the divine mystery supreme. A wonderful thing it is and the source of our happiness. We need not wait to see what others do.

This quote reminds me of when I was a child watching cartoons. I remember the image during a variety of cartoons of a little devil with a pitchfork and an angel with a halo standing on either side of the character battling for influence over the situation. Tom and Jerry is one that I recall. I see this image in my head when I read about this "still small voice" that we often call conscience or inner voice. It is important that we strengthen this inner voice and, of course, choose the halo over the pitchfork. Stephen R. Covey wrote a follow up book to the *7 Habits of Highly Effective People* entitled [1] *The 8th Habit: From Effectiveness to Greatness* in which he promotes this idea of finding your voice and helping others to find theirs. He teaches that independence is important and a prerequisite to effective interdependence. He points out that we really want to go from "Good to Great;" therefore, the next step in our journey starts with us finding that inner voice of purpose and passion and its intersection with others.

This leads well into the paragraph excerpt from Gandhi that is thought to be where we get the statement of "we must be the change you want to see in the world." We are interconnected and we cannot separate the work we do within and its impact without. We must work to change ourselves by intentional choice and develop our tools to consistently seek a life of meaning that promotes unity within ourselves as we contribute to the world outside of ourselves. Your leading of yourself will impact your leading in your home, job/vocation, friendships, church, and other places you live, move, and have your being. Often, circumstances can overwhelm and get frustrating. Have you ever heard, "this world's going to hell in a hand basket?" I have often looked around and wondered who is going to lead us through this or that. I have looked upon recent leadership realities with less and less hope, but I know that the only way things will change is if I become an influencer of those changes I want to see. Significant change occurs by influencing the next generation in ways that promote the change we want to see. "We need not wait to see what others do..." All the noise and confusion around us is not what matters. What matters is our response to it all. You can't change every circumstance of the world but you can change you. May we work hard to develop the right leading that sees the development of self as the first step to the right contributions to the world in which we live. Every day, before you really begin to interact with the world outside, take care of nourishing your world inside. Lead.

> *"Wherefore, my beloved, as ye have always obeyed, not as in my presence only, but now much more in my absence, work out your own salvation with fear and trembling. For it is God which worketh in you both to will and to do of his good pleasure"*

— PHILIPPIANS 2:12-13 KJV

"Perfect valor is to do without witness what one would do before all the world."

— LA ROCHEFOUCAULD

Many people define this unity between the voice of conscience (assuming the voice speaks truth) and the actions of life as integrity. After all, nobody can really see inside your conscience or hear the speaking of your "still small voice." Like La Rochefoucauld, many say integrity is what you do when no one is watching. I would argue integrity is much deeper. Integrity requires consistent application and is evident in the open and in the private. The most cancerous act negating integrity is lying to yourself. I believe integrity is all about the integration of Spirit, Soul (mind, will, emotions), and Body into a unified self that is made for this designed world. We lead ourselves into a life worth living by staying true to a principle-centered leadership character. We build a life that is worth living like an artist builds a sculpture out of an un-shaped rock of raw material. Integrity comes from the word integrate. I often use a simple activity with the hands to demonstrate my basic view of integrity. I ask an individual to open both hands and identify one hand as important core beliefs and values. I then have the person take the other hand and identify it as actions and words. Lastly, I have them bring the hands together with unification at the base of the finger joint so there is no space between the hands and the fingers are able to grasp one another to hold together the right and the left. Integrity is when our right hand of beliefs and values absolutely knows what the left hand of action and execution is doing and the two hands align as one. Leading yourself with integrity is essentially being who you think and say you are, while working to close the gap between what you know to be timeless principles and your actions of living them out. Mark Rutland said that "the most basic values held by a society dictate the kind of leaders it will produce." What will your leadership of self and others produce? Do your values and your actions match? None of us can say "yes" 100% of the time, but integrity requires effort in doing the work to make it so.

> "The integrity of the upright guides them, but the unfaithful are destroyed by their duplicity"

— PROVERBS 11:3 NIV

> "Every block of stone has a sculpture inside of it and it is the task of the sculptor to discover it."

— MICHELANGELO

A blank slate of rock already holds the sculpture, but the artist's vision has to see more than a mere rock. Your life is a masterpiece you live and this life integrates principles you must envision for execution into the final form of excellence. Vision usually precedes provision. "Measure twice, cut once." Vision ignites passion and purpose toward an end or WHY worthy of completing at a level considered "well done" or excellent. Without a vision, efforts fail, people perish, but with vision and a clear "end in mind," clarification comes to the chiseling of stone that shapes our statue into a meaningful result. Consider the chainsaw artist at the fair. I spent over an hour watching an artist at the fair in Marietta. I watched as he began with this blank log and I already had confidence in his skills as I could see masterpieces of his handiwork on display around his work tent. He starts with this pine log and a bunch of tools (chain saws of various sizes and wood chisels) and begins cutting and trimming the parts of the wood away that are not needed for the end or vision in his mind of this great eagle or bear or whatever. He is intentional and focused on this end and he chooses the saw based on the task to cut at the right angle and pressure to remove excess first and then to fine tune the sculpting into the finer points of wings, holes in the beak, and claws on a limb.

In our life, we must have a vision (personal mission statement) of what excellence looks like to us. The potential for a beautiful work of art is within a block of granite, a cord of wood, or even a blank canvas ready for paint. Bob Ross is another artist that I've spent hours watching using his sunny disposition to teach others how to paint these scenes we often see in nature. How does he do it? He sees in his mind's eye before he even begins putting brush to paint and paint to canvas. He even discovers that mistakes in his strokes yield opportunities to adjust the vision in his mind and change the flow of art in his hands as he integrates his sight with the strokes of his hand and the mindful selections of paint colors. What a beautiful metaphor for life, and this thing we call vision. Can I see in my mind's eye the outcomes of my life and intentionally adjust my strokes to complete a masterpiece that, when I'm done, I will be happy to share with those around me?

> *"And the LORD answered me, and said, Write the vision, and make it plain upon tables, that he may run that readeth it."*
>
> — HABAKKUK 2:2 KJV

> *"Where there is no vision, the people perish: but he that keepeth the law, happy is he."*
>
> — PROVERBS 29:18 KJV

> "The quality of a man's life is in direct proportion to his commitment to excellence, regardless of his chosen field of endeavor."
>
> — VINCE LOMBARDI

THE TROPHY that NFL players dream of holding is named after the man who penned the aforementioned statement. Abraham Lincoln said it simply, "Whatever you are, be a good one." I find the most difficult mud to get out of is where I settle because I'm doing better than many or most around me. Am I content to stand and let my feet settle in the mud or am I willing to do the work and move toward the pinnacle of the best version of myself I can be? Along this journey, somehow, I find that me becoming me influences directly and indirectly others becoming themselves. The first person I influence is me, but when I do that in excellence (excel), I influence others as well. Sometimes we overcomplicate the simple and glorify complexity when it's not necessary. Three stepping stones to excellence are perseverance, simplicity and balance. Tom Peters describes a life of perseverance and simplicity in the following passage: "Life is pretty simple. You do some stuff. Most fail. Some work. You do more of what works. If it works big, others quickly copy it. Then you do something else."

How often do we see or hear of inventions, thoughts, or creations from others we know were dreams within us? The magic happens in the doing. The root of perseverance persists. Keep getting after it. Don't quit. There is a Japanese Proverb that says, "Fall seven times, stand up eight." Simplicity is required to gain focus and to be able to finish what you start. Ashleigh Brilliant was brilliant in saying "I can do only one thing at a time, but I can avoid doing many things simultaneously." Learn to simplify the focus of your energy by saying "no" over and over so you can give appropriate energy to the right "yes." Balance is all about allocating time and energy to the right "stuff" and making the most of your moments. Stephen R. Covey said, "To make the best use of time, we need to live each moment as it is vitally important." Hugh Mulligan said "what I do today is important because I am exchanging a day of my life for it." How we balance our roles in life and the time we allocate to the tasks we deem important defines this life of balance. "The future is purchased by the present" (Samual Johnson.) What are you purchasing with your present choices and the excellence of your action? True living is leading your life in such a way where natural laws and godly principles not only influence you, but are integrated into your being. Dr. Myles Munroe said that leadership is "becoming yourself so that you may benefit others." May we decide today, tomorrow, and the next to lead ourselves with integrity. May we work diligently to examine the whole person of who we are spirit, soul, and body. May our work directly and proportionately develop a meaningful vision of excellence so the process of growth, change, or "becoming" produces fruit to fuel ourselves and the people we influence.

> *"He that hath knowledge spareth his words: and a man of understanding is of an excellent spirit."*
>
> — PROVERBS 17:27 KJV

> *"That ye may approve things that are excellent; that ye may be sincere and without offence till the day of Christ,"*
>
> — PHILIPPIANS 1:10 KJV

7

LIVE WITH INTENT AND FAITHFULNESS TOWARD EXECUTION!

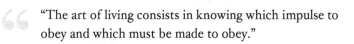

"The art of living consists in knowing which impulse to obey and which must be made to obey."

— SYDNEY J. HARRIS

As we go about life, it is often frustrating (and even depressing) to find ourselves failing to execute around the goals and activities that make our life matter. The essence of a good life is one where we feel we obey the right voices and the screaming inner voice of purpose is never muffled by the demands of impulses outside our lane. Knowing your lane and staying in it is what life is about. My personal mission statement is to "Lead people who matter to do things that matter." We all want to give energy to things in our lives that matter. We all want to make a difference and impact the world around us, including its people. We should desire to be influencers. We should also be humble enough to be influenced. People should always be the priority. Our activity and pursuits should always be weighed and valued based on how they impact the most important people in our lives. We hear people talk about time management, behavior modification, and motivation. I believe these types of conversations often lead to more confusion. Time cannot be managed. It is simply a combination of measurements of gravitational pull on the earth and discernments of earth's rotation and orbital patterns creating meaningful conditions for our existence. Night and day, seasons, etc., are all results of these measurements of which "time" is a primary describer. We cannot impact time one bit, but we can impact what we do during the seasons and moments with which we exist and interact. Live on purpose for people.

> *"The thief cometh not, but for to steal, and to kill, and to destroy:*
> *I am come that they might have life, and that they might*
> *have it more abundantly."*

— JOHN 10:10 KJV

"Time flies, but, remember you're the navigator."

— ST. LOUIS BUGLE

What we give our attention to reveals intentionality. We have the power to choose our attitudes and actions. We can't control all life's circumstances but we can control our response. Stephen R. Covey says "make your own weather." Behavioral modification would not be necessary if we took full responsibility for our impact on what matters to us by carefully discerning our intent along with the causation of results governed by actions we choose. Motives exist in everything we say and do, but like emotions, they can quickly change due to their fickle nature and the influencers all around. Motivation is fine, but mission is meatier. Time, behavior, and motivation are all three servants to a greater trio of activity: purpose, character (habits), and mission (passionate pursuit of purpose.) Be intentional about the activities you participate in, the character and habits you are forming, and the missions you intend to complete. If we are honest with ourselves, we will find that this LIFE acronym is all about where the rubber meets the road. Living in this environment of clocks, seasons, and terrain requires intentional thought when we desire to live on purpose or on mission and we really do recognize the value of our endowments to influence and be influenced. We are the master of our destiny. Our thoughts, speech, and actions determine what we build, where we go, and ultimately what monument our chiseled stone becomes. We must learn to live with intent. We must decide our choices and actions matter. Living on purpose means we are intentional about what we think about, talk about, and why we do what we do. Our mission is always in view and our energies are concentrated on what really matters to us.

> *"See then that ye walk circumspectly, not as fools, but as wise, Redeeming the time, because the days are evil. Wherefore be ye not unwise, but understanding what the will of the Lord is."*
>
> — EPHESIANS 5:15-17 KJV

 "Faithfulness is God's plumb line."

> — GENE EVANS

How many times do we find ourselves focusing on something and getting a good start, but not a real finish? This is where the word faithfulness comes. I think of faithfulness as trustworthy and dependable. As stewards of our gifts, talents, and energy, we determine if we will apply the right energy to the right things or if we lose focus and forget what matters. The L.I.F.E. acronym is a reminder to us that we need to live and move with intentional focus and faithful execution toward worthy ends. If it's worth doing, it's worth doing right and worth doing consistently. Faithful people do what they say. Faithful people show up on time. Faithful people show up consistently. Faithful people are dependable. Gene Evans, my pastor for 18 years often said, "Faithfulness is God's plumb line." His messages on faithfulness greatly influenced the value I place on this principle in my life.

Faithfulness is required in the following three areas:

1. The little things – Have you ever heard, "The devil's in the details?" It's the little things that build the foundation for

the big things. "He that is faithful in that which is least if faithful also in much." (Jesus, Jewish Carpenter and Christian Messiah) Mother Teresa said, "Be faithful in small things because it is in them that your strength lies."

2. That which is another man's – How often do we see great leadership birthed from a mentored relationship from another great leader? The most consistent way to build effectiveness in skilled workers is through apprenticeship, not degree programs. When we learn and work beside a skilled person, we often acquire similar skills and possibly even learn from their mistakes to build greater skill. Serving another and being influenceable by others is a great foundation for growth and excellence. Being a champion for another's business, vision, or goal often helps you build a foundation or platform to build your legacy. Always work to be found faithful with the trust given to you by others in their work and/or property.

3. Money, things, the stuff – We must learn to be faithful with money, capital, our own natural tools and resources such as vehicles, etc. before we can be entrusted with true riches that surpass material wealth and riches. Being able to rule your money instead of money ruling you or being able to rule your fashion rather than to be trapped in what is fashionable is a good barometer of success. The quickest things that reveal bad character are the obvious abuses of stealing money or wasting money through failed stewardship of the resources that make you money. Be faithful in the little things, that which is currently another's, and your money and stuff, and the Law of the Harvest will pay out greatly in your life.

"Moreover it is required in stewards, that a man be found faithful."

— I CORINTHIANS 4:2 KJV

"He that is faithful in that which is least is faithful also in much: and he that is unjust in the least is unjust also in much. If therefore ye have not been faithful in the unrighteous mammon, who will commit to your trust the true riches? And if ye have not been faithful in that which is another man's, who shall give you that which is your own?"

— LUKE 16:10-12 KJV

 "You can't build a reputation on what you're going to do."

— HENRY FORD

Henry Ford recognized that execution is the key to growth and prosperity in business and in life. You can't talk your way out of problems you behave into yourselves. Benjamin Franklin said, "Well done is better than well said." Toby Keith sings, "A little less talk, if you please, a lot more action is what I need." We already established the importance of intent and faithfulness which feeds perfectly into your plan's execution. I once read a book by authors within Franklin Covey called *The 4 Disciplines of Execution*. This book gave emphasis to the prevailing concern relevant in business that we often do the work of vision casting, mission mindset, and goal-setting and still experience failure because of execution. I would argue some of that is due to a lack of faithfulness with the little things and "big rocks" of our organization. We often fail to establish good intent and faithfulness resulting in the misalignment of the fruits of execution within the actual mission and/or vision. The 4DX concept is worth the read as it points out 4 key components to keep alive during the execution phase[1].

These components are focus, leverage, engagement and accountability.

1. Focus on the Wildly Important Goals (WIGs.) Set meaningful goals that are worthy of your energy and effort.
2. Work on the lead measures: Find the meaningful lead

measures to increase what you want to multiply or decrease what you want to omit. Measure what matters.

3. Keep a compelling score card. The most powerful visual during a televised game is the scoreboard in the corner that tells the spectator the score and all other relevant measures. Measure what matters and keep it before you.

4. Create a rhythm of accountability: Create opportunities to revisit the scoreboard and evaluate why we are where we are and how we can punctuate the successes (celebrate) and mitigate risks and failure. Execution is often the sticky phase.

When I set a goal to run my first 50K in the mountains of North Georgia, I thought I had prepared myself, but I underestimated the significance of the challenge in relation to time and elevation. I couldn't run the distance fast enough to make cutoffs and the elevation was my biggest factor. I had a vision, a mission, a strong work ethic and a good team to assist me. My execution failed once, but I succeeded on my second attempt. To execute, I had to be intentional about my eating, cross-training workouts, and running. I had to "practice how you play" and purposefully train on the terrain that I would run during the race. I had to be intentional about the types of runs I spent time doing and faithful to the timeline when my execution was necessary. Prior to my second attempt, I ran multiple 20-plus mile training missions including two on the Duncan Ridge Trail. I did a birthday run/hike of 25 miles on the trail and a follow up run of 22 miles at Berry College the next day to truly challenge my endurance and my mental toughness. That was a milestone challenge in itself (47 miles for my 47th birthday.) Almost all such runs were done with similar elevation and terrain as DRT 50K (my Wildly Important Goal.) These runs and the metrics of the runs became my work on the lead measures. My compelling score card was the planning of these special long runs, and the stored information in my "Connect" app recorded my pace and elevation for each mission. My cadence of accountability was documenting a training schedule and revisiting my micro-goals along the way. My accountability was to myself and my closest friends including my wife and daughter who would crew me the day of the race. The race was rainy and the course was much slower due to the increased mud, but I had trained more than enough to prepare myself for these challenges. In life, we will run into opportunities for failure and we often learn more from them than we do from success. May we remember to live (move and do things) with intent and faithfulness that match the intended outcomes we want to gain and execute consistently on mission relevant initiatives. Live with intent and faithfulness toward execution.

> *"For as the body without the spirit is dead, so faith without works is dead also."*
>
> — JAMES 2:26 KJV

> *"But be ye doers of the word, and not hearers only, deceiving your own selves."*
>
> — JAMES 1:22 KJV

8

LOVE OTHERS UNCONDITIONALLY THROUGH DIVINE INFLUENCE!

"In this life we cannot do great things. We can only do small things with great love."

— MOTHER TERESA

"Jesus said unto him, Thou shalt love the Lord thy God with all thy heart, and with all thy soul, and with all thy mind. This is the first and great commandment. And the second is like unto it, Thou shalt love thy neighbor as thyself. On these two commandments hang all the law and the prophets."

— MATTHEW 22:37-40 KJV

Society rings out this notion of "good to great" and the passion to do or be great. Mother Teresa is a very inspirational and influential person due to her ability to live out the acronym I've penned here. There is so much in this world where we find meaning and so much where we do not. There is very little meaning to be found in material wealth and the stuff we can accumulate. We know "You can't take it with you." There is value in money, shelter over your head, vehicles for travel, and clothing that functions effectively.

Material wealth, in itself, is not evil or wrong. The love of money or material; however, could be a problem. I love this last acronym because I think it really hits on a most important truth that cannot be denied or skirted in life. There is so much in this life that is bigger than "self." I heard a story related by Dr. Henry Cloud about a woman who was constantly visiting her psychiatrist and spending hours in therapy complaining about her life with the pronouns "me" and "I". The therapist eventually wrote her a prescription which totally threw her for a loop. He wrote a prescription for a trip to the Grand Canyon. Upon asking why he would write such a prescription, he told her that she needed to discover in her life things much bigger than herself. Oh, that we could discover this truth about a Creator who fearfully and wonderfully designed us.

Perhaps we can even discover what happens to us may be part of a design as well. I had an "aha" moment when reading a scripture that articulates this one commandment that summarizes to me this acronym, "Love the Lord your God with all of your heart, soul, mind, and strength and your neighbor as yourself." The context of this scripture is a Jewish Carpenter, who had garnered quite an audience, speaking to his top followers. He gave this as the greatest commandment and when one of his followers asked, "Who is my neighbor?" Jesus told the story of "The Good Samaritan." This story was of a Samaritan who became the unlikely benefactor of a stranger beaten and left for dead. He even took him to an inn and paid for his stay and treatment and promised to pay any bills that accrued. It's fairly accepted that we should treat others as we desire to be treated. Martin Luther King, Jr. said, "Love is the only force powerful enough to transform an enemy into a friend."

Dare we believe that we should love others unconditionally? Is there any way that we could be unselfish enough to think of others before ourselves. Some of our conventional behaviors of courtesy imply such sentiment such as opening or holding the door for strangers, speaking to others with statements like, "Good day, mate," or picking up trash others dropped off their tray. We call them "Random acts of kindness" or "Pay it forward." There are so many ways in which we can live out this virtuous acronym, but I would argue that you cannot do so without help from Divine influence. We must recognize that all of creation is special and there is a Creator or Designer giving us the basis for every bit of meaning we seek in this life. Loving God may look different based on your belief system, but I doubt it possible to live and lead well without some revelation of a higher power and a great conscience that inspires us to care more for others than we do for ourselves. The revelation I gained in the scripture quoted above was to recognize and love our Creator first.

We don't really know who we are outside of the context of His Design. Secondly, we can't love others without recognizing the implication of the portion of scripture that states, "as thyself." If you don't value and respect yourself and the gifts and talents you possess, how could you possibly shift to a meaningful investment in the lives of others? If you think you're trash and not worth much, how will that play out in its impact on others? Loving others and being willing to listen enough to try to gain understanding of others' challenges and needs will take you to a "whole nother" level of being that transcends your simple daily victory over your own challenges. Certainly, win first in you, but invest yourself in the winning of others. Find those win/win opportunities and exploit them for your good as well as the good of others. We all share a lot of the same tools and resources. We are all complex spiritual beings in a dirt "earth suit" if you will, but ultimately we are all in this thing called life and we are truly better together. LIVE LIFE LOUD by leading with integrity around a vision for excellence. Live with intent and faithfulness toward execution around things that really matter. Be a doer because that's what you intended and love others unconditionally through Divine influence.

> *"For in Jesus Christ neither circumcision availeth anything, nor uncircumcision; but faith which worketh by love."*
>
> — GALATIANS 5:6 KJV

> *"If I could speak all the languages of earth and of angels, but didn't love others, I would only be a noisy gong or a clanging cymbal. If I had the gift of prophecy, and if I understood all*

of God's secret plans and possessed all knowledge, and if I had such faith that I could move mountains, but didn't love others, I would be nothing. If I gave everything I have to the poor and even sacrificed my body, I could boast about it, but if I didn't love others, I would have gained nothing. Love is patient and kind. Love is not jealous or boastful or proud or rude. It does not demand its own way. It is not irritable, and it keeps no record of being wronged. It does not rejoice about injustice but rejoices whenever the truth wins out. Love never gives up, never loses faith, is always hopeful, and endures through every circumstance,"

— I CORINTHIANS 13:1-7 NLT

III

SPIRIT LED, SOUL FED, BODY DEAD

B.E.S.T. LIFE AHEAD!

As a young child, my mom devoured books and her favorite was the Bible. She bought new bibles in nearly every translation. When she acquired a new translation, she would sit down with a notebook and write about things she learned. She also journaled in these notebooks about topics of study. These notebooks rested in a laundry basket and we often joked about the fact that, if the house ever caught fire, we should probably make sure we got that laundry basket full of years and years of notes. Mom taught me to value scripture. The first major book I read cover to cover was the King James Bible. I would sit in church when the preaching was not inspiring me and read the Bible so I could finish.

At a young age, I memorized scripture and studied deeply the meaning of Greek and Hebrew words that were underlined in my Greek and Hebrew Study Bible. Mom exposed me to a variety of Christian authors, but one of my favorites was Myles Munroe. Everything he wrote seemed to go back to purpose. He taught me purpose was found in the operator's manual and that our manual was the Holy Bible. I remember reading Genesis 1 and 2 over and over again and studying the words used to come to this realization that, as God formed Adam out of the dust of the earth, He breathed the breath of life into him and Adam became a living soul. I studied deeply to learn that Adam was formed in dirt and given spiritual life from God's breath. This made sense to me based on the origins of the word human. Humus is dirt and man is spirit meaning a human is spirit in dirt. This was also a teaching that Dr. Myles Munroe reinforced in his writings. I suppose we are all interested in the beginnings of man and the design of creation.

I believed at a young age that anything I needed to know would ultimately be found in the owner's manual because John 1:1 said, "in the beginning was the Word and the Word was with God and the Word was God." John 6:63 tells us the flesh profits nothing but God's Word is Spirit and It is life. I began to develop my understanding that we are made in the image of a Triune God: Father, Son, and Holy Spirit. We are also a triune being. We are a spirit, we have a soul, and we live in a body. This revelation occurred to me prior to my teen years, but I began voicing my beliefs in college. After a deep conversation with my philosophy professor at Berry College, I felt I had a good grasp of my life's purpose as a result of this realization. This whole Christian life became my journey of living out Romans 12:1-2. "I beseech ye..." I wanted to be transformed in how I thought and interacted in the physical world. Two scriptures speak to the essence on how this whole slogan reads. Paul teaches the Corinthian church in his letter that "...if any man be in Christ, he is a new creature: old things are passed away; behold, all things are become new." I believe the moment we believe in our hearts and confess with our mouth the truth about Jesus and His work on the cross for us, we become a new being, alive with the resurrection life of Christ. We go through a renewal and build an integrated trinity of spirit, soul, and body where we work out this salvation that was purchased for us.

In Philippians 2:12, Paul encourages the church to "work out your own salvation with fear and trembling." This working out is taught in many ways throughout the New Testament. We are to put on Christ and put off the fruitless works of darkness. We are to be renewed in the spirit of our mind and prove the good, acceptable and perfect will of God (Romans 12:2.) I truly believe we have the life of God available to us through the work of the cross and our friend, Holy Spirit, who comes to reveal truth so we can be led by Him. We receive understanding and grow in the knowledge of God so our soul (mind, will, and emotions) is able to convert the spiritual life of the Word of God into meaningful expressions of principle-centered living that is carried out in the body. This idea of Spirit Led, Soul Fed, Body Dead is a biblical look at a discipleship journey of living "in earth as it is in heaven" our best life. We will look at what each part of the trinity of man means for us and how the integration of our spirit, soul, and body into an obedient servant will lead to our best life.

9

THE TRINITY OF MAN: INTEGRATION OF SPIRIT, SOUL, AND BODY

> "For as many as are led by the Spirit of God, they are the sons of God."

— ROMANS 8:14 KJV

SPIRIT LED

What is spirit? The word in the Old Testament is "ruwah" and in the New Testament it is "pneuma." Both are basically defined as breath. We use the term pneumatic drill to describe a tool that is powered by breath or air. Spirit is basically the substance of life in the form of air making us a living being. The apostle Paul tells us in Romans that the flesh is warring against the spirit and the spirit against the flesh so what I want to do, I don't and what I don't want to do, I do. A reading of the seventh chapter of Romans reveals this articulation of a war waging in this body of sin we are living in; however, there is a solution in chapter eight. Romans 8 is the chapter that tells us that we are no longer under condemnation if we are in Christ Jesus. The law of the spirit of life in Christ Jesus has freed us from the evil desires that consistently cause us to miss the target of right living. We are no longer under the burden of sin because our right-standing with God was purchased by the brutal crucifixion, and Christ's resurrection life (verse II) is able to dwell in us and make our mortal bodies alive. Paul tells us that, if we are led by the Spirit, we will not fulfill the evil desires of the flesh and the battle is won. Jesus' words in John 6:63 say the flesh profits us nothing, but that His Words are Spirit and they are life.

In order to be Spirit led, we must be led by the truth of the Word of God. Proverbs 4: 20-24 admonishes us to "attend to" God's word and "incline thine ears" to his sayings, keeping them in our hearts for the Word is life and health to "all their flesh." Joshua 1:8 is a passage that teaches Joshua how to lead. Joshua is taking over the leadership of the Israelites and this passage tells him to make sure "this book of the law" doesn't depart from his mouth but he should meditate in it day and night so he can "observe to do according to all that is written." The guarantee is that, if he does this, he will make his way prosperous and experience success. There are so many things that happen in this world we cannot understand or explain. Being led by the Holy Spirit of God is not some strange phenomenon where people roll around on the floor and foam at the mouth and play with rattlesnakes. This being "Spirit Led" is an opportunity to allow the life of God through His gracious gift to, by faith, enable us to gain insight into an invisible world of His will in a way that produces fruit unto right living. We have this treasure of His life in us and in our "earthen vessels" to be His ambassadors. We are told in the book of John we are no longer called servants because servants don't get the direct link to the master plan, but we are friends because He reveals his purposes and plans to us through the Spirit. Isaiah teaches us that His ways are higher than our ways and His thoughts higher than our thoughts, but in the New Testament, I Corinthians 2:16, "we have the mind of Christ." This mind is only accessible through the work of the indwelling of the Spirit of God. We are called to be Spirit Led which should influence our mind, our mouth, and our movement.

3 M'S MIND-MOUTH-MOVEMENT

> *"For as he thinketh in his heart, so is he: Eat and drink, saith he to thee; but his heart is not with thee."*

— PROVERBS 23:7 KJV

"Keep your heart with all diligence; for out of it are the issues of life."

— PROVERBS 4:23 KJV

"A good man out of the good treasure of his heart bringeth forth that which is good; and an evil man out of the evil treasure of his heart bringeth forth that which is evil: for of the abundance of the heart his mouth speaketh."

— LUKE 6:45 KJV

"For verily I say unto you, That whosoever shall say unto this mountain, Be thou removed, and be thou cast into the sea; and shall not doubt in his heart, but shall believe that those things which he saith shall come to pass; he shall have whatsoever he saith. Therefore I say unto you, What things soever ye desire, when ye pray, believe that ye receive them and ye shall have them."

— MARK 11:23-24 KJV

Let's consider this concept of being Spirit Led so we can be influenced in our mind, our mouth, and our movement. The scriptures that open this section are fundamental teachings on the power of our thinking and how thinking influences our heart, which then influences our mouth. The power of the spoken word is important because "we have what we say." In the early 1900s, a man by the name of James Allen wrote *As a Man Thinketh* in which he communicates the power of our mind and our thought life. This book is not about Biblical teaching, but about the power of our thought life and how this influences our ability to be in harmony with nature and our own human nature. The power of our thought life is evident in the teaching of people who emphasize "mindfulness" or self-improvement "meditation."

These Biblical concepts revealed in Proverbs, Luke, and Mark are perpetuated throughout secular ideas like "the law of attraction" and a variety of humanistic philosophies. People who do not claim any allegiance to God or a specific religion know there are principles in play that relate to the power of our mind and mouth to produce fruit in our movement that inspires creation to cooperate and give us "good success." I believe God made all we know and understand and His plan is to reveal all He can to His people so we are able to be good stewards of His creation and use what we know and say to move into His plan for our good. In order to be led by the Spirit, we must listen with the intent to gain knowledge, understanding, and wisdom so, in obedience, we can live how we are designed. Since we have the Designer's life in us, we get to choose to think right, talk right, and live right. This influences the 3 M's of our mind, mouth, and movement. The ultimate truth of our triune being is that the Spirit is who we are. The food which sustains a spirit being is spiritual food. That food is the Word of God which is spirit and life. To live this life well, you must be led and fed by the Spirit of His life.

SOUL FED

> *"And be renewed in the spirit of your mind; And that ye put on
> the new man, which after God is created in righteousness
> and true holiness"*

— EPHESIANS 4:23-24 KJV

There is a great confusion regarding the differences between certain terms such as soul, heart, spirit. There are crossover meanings in these words because, as a human, you are a spirit, you have a soul, and you live in a body. Missing one of these components of the trinity of man leaves us incomplete. In the Old Testament, the word for soul is "nephesh" and the New Testament word is "psuche." The word "nephesh" means a breathing creature. The word "pschē" means breath or life. The implication according to Strong's Concordance is the soul is the seat of human feelings and emotions. The soul is often interchangeable with the word heart because they both tend to reveal the innermost thoughts and feelings. There is no clean way to dissect this word without an understanding of the life of the spirit breath and the power of this breath indwelling the human body so the mind, will, and emotions of man are his soul. Man's psychological make up is not simply a spiritual wind or breath, but there is a part of our human person that is free to choose (will) and demonstrate emotions based on the work of the mind. This soul and spirit distinction is demonstrated well by Paul in his first letter to the Corinthian church in chapter fifteen, verse forty-five. The King James Version reads, "And so it is written, The first man Adam was made a living soul; the last Adam was made a quickening spirit." Christ was made unto us a quickening breath, but we already have a living substance of breath in us that is the seat of our mind, will, and emotions.

Consider the people who demonstrate an unexplainable will to live in circumstances that would certainly mean death for most. This overcoming nature or will is in all living creatures and is emboldened and strengthened by the challenges of life. Just as a person challenges his/her muscles to do more and more through specific exercises to produce a breaking down and tribulation, the completion of these adverse conditions have a training effect that causes the muscles to adapt and overcome by growing stronger and more resilient. It is important for us to be certain we nourish our soul with the right work and nutrients so we build a strong, resilient seat of mind, will, and emotions from which to operate.

God breathed the breath of life into Adam and he became a living soul. When Adam sinned, he was separated from that life because of disobedience and Jesus, the second Adam, became a "quickening spirit." That life provided by Jesus' work on Calvary was not a destruction of the law and the principles communicated in the law for man to live by. This completed work on Calvary was a fulfillment of what we could not do because we are weak in our flesh. What we could not do in our flesh because of the messed up state of our psyche, Christ did. He provided access to a life we were denied through Adam's disobedience. Christ's obedience in becoming sin on our behalf, freed us from the law of sin and death and made us a new creature in Christ. This work is a miracle of pneuma (spirit breath) coming into our human spirit in a way that wants to have permission to express itself in our life. Romans 12:1-2 gives us the formula for renewal of our mind so we can demonstrate an outward expression that is consistent with the life of God we were given access to by the Holy Spirit being sent to do this work in us. Consider this translation of Romans 12:1-2 from [1]Kenneth Wuest. "I therefore beg of you, please, brethren, through the instrumentality of the aforementioned mercies of God, by a once-for-all presentation to place your bodies at the disposal of God, a sacrifice, a living one, a holy one, well-pleasing, your rational, sacred service, [rational, in that this service is performed by the exercise of the mind]. And stop assuming an outward expression that does not come from within you and is not representative of your inner being but is patterned after this age; but change your outward expression to one that comes from within and is representative of your inner being, by the renewing of your mind, resulting in your putting to the test what is the will of God, the good and well-pleasing and complete will, and having found that it meets specifications, place your approval upon it," (The New Testament - An Expanded Translation.)

I know this passage is full of long, run-on sentences that require a great deal of meditation and focus, but let's consider some of the "expansion" in text and see if it resonates. We are asked by Paul to present our bodies as a living sacrifice through an exercise of the mind. Regardless of the translation, we are encouraged to "be transformed by the renewing of our mind." The purpose of this renewal is to stop living outside of integrity where we are not expressing in how we talk, live, and walk the realities of this new creation we claim has occurred through the breath of the Spirit. Paul teaches us we are to "work out" our salvation. If we are saved by grace through faith, what is being "worked out?" We are working out the transformation of having our mind, will, and emotions renewed to the truth of the Word of God so our soul is living again.

Do you find yourself thinking erratically and in ways that do not produce a peaceful life? Do you ever think thoughts like, "If I'm saved and a new creation, why do I not always do what God wants me to do even when I think that I want to be obedient?" There is a battle going on in your person where the flesh is at war with the spirit and you are constantly trying to fight. You have evil desires in your flesh that want to have what makes you feel good consistently become your reward . At the same time, there are disciplines of self-control that want to win out and cause you to obey the Word of God. There is this battle between the standards of truth in the Word of God and in good counsel versus the "if it feels good, do it" flesh cry. We are constantly in this war and the battle rages in our mind or our soul. You are a spiritual being, but you live in an earth suit that gives you access to multiple tools such as the five physical senses of seeing, hearing, feeling (touch), smelling, and tasting. These senses are so integrated that oftentimes one impacts the other.

Take, for example, taste. Our like or dislike of food is primarily on taste; however, texture (feeling or touch) and smell impact the interpretation of our taste buds. Two different people like or dislike the same item based on various combinations based on this feedback. All of these components of senses and the interpretation of them are specific mechanisms of the body. If part of the body that performs the receptive function of any of these senses gets damaged, the sense can be lost. Sometimes the loss of sense is in the brain, sometimes it is in the receptivity of the organ itself. For instance, a person who has lost their eyesight may have lost an eye or suffered damage in the functioning of the eye. Some folks suffer vision problems through a traumatic brain injury where all of the tissues of the eye are healthy and intact. There is this beautiful connectivity between the brain, spinal column, and organs in the body that have tissues that perform functions to enable these complex senses. Are the interpretation of these senses performed in the body or the soul? Are the brain and mind synonyms? What are the different functions of each? The brain interprets information and houses the emotions, will, and intellect to some degree. Research of the human brain allows us to know with high degrees of certainty where particular functions of the brain occur including logic, reasoning, right-side movement, left-side movement, reflexes, emotional response, etc. I would argue that the spirit, soul, and body are to be integrated and that without any one component, the other components cannot serve a useful function on earth. The soul serves as the bridge or gatekeeper between the body and spirit so the will or "want to" for obedience to the life of the spirit and the power to say "no" to the correct impulses that try to war with what is right resides in the transformation of the soul. Spirit led people have to be guided at the helm of the soul through the renewal of a mind that is continuously growing in the knowledge of God. The idea of Soul Fed is this transformation where the mind is renewed to see the word of God which, according to John 6:63 is spirit and life. The flesh profits nothing, but a soul that is fed will bring the truth of spiritual life into the earthen vessel of man where the word has impact on our flesh (Proverbs 4:23.) A person that is "Spirit Led" will choose to be "Soul Fed" according to Romans 12:2 so there is a fleshing out of the truth of God's word. Obedience is better than sacrifice. Faith without works is dead. Soulish renewal and keeping of the gate is the key aspect of human influence over spiritual relationship. We don't get to save ourselves. We don't get to make decisions that are God's to make. We do; however, get to choose by our own will whether we will choose life or death, blessings or cursing, right or wrong, victory or defeat, faith or fear. Choose this day, whom you will serve. Choose to be spirit led and soul fed. Renew your mind by the Word of God and the principles of Godly wisdom that cause you to be like the man who built his house upon a rock so when the winds and storm came, this man's house endured.

To conclude this principle of being soul fed, remember the wisdom of Solomon, in Proverbs 23:7 who said that "as a man thinketh in his heart, so is he." Consider Paul's encouragement to "be renewed in the spirit of your mind" and "be transformed by the renewing of your mind" so you can be proof providers. We are not our own saviors, but we do determine the working out of this great salvation in our lives by choosing to feed the soul, renew the mind, and allow the Word of God to save our souls. Wherefore lay apart all filthiness and superfluity of naughtiness, and receive with meekness the engrafted word, which is able to save your souls. The book of James specifically admonishes us to be doers of the word.

Wherefore lay apart all filthiness and superfluity of naughtiness,
and receive with meekness the engrafted word, which is able

to save your souls 22 But be ye doers of the word, and not
hearers only, deceiving your own selves. 23 For if any be a
hearer of the word, and not a doer, he is like unto a man
beholding his natural face in a glass: 24 For he beholdeth
himself, and goeth his way, and straightway forgetteth what
manner of man he was.

— JAMES 1:21-24 KJV

From this passage we gain several important insights into this idea of being "Soul Fed." The author tells us to get rid of actions that are naughty and "receive with meekness the engrafted word." I believe we have to receive with meekness because there is power in His Word that we are not able to uphold in arrogance and without demonstrating a servant-like character. After all, John 1:1 tells us that Jesus, our best example of a servant leader, is the Word. The word "engrafted" indicates that it is "imparted by nature" and this impartation will save our souls. We must be motivated to push away a lifestyle that is filthy or naughty and be ready to experience a renewal in our soul by this word that is imparted by the very nature of the truth of the word itself. The process of becoming a proof provider, a disciple of Christ, a "little anointed one," as the word Christian implies, requires we do the work of receiving this word. That is the essence of being "Soul Fed." The next step is also found in this passage as the integration of "Soul Fed" to "Body Dead" is demonstrated in a fruitful life of doing what He commands.

BODY DEAD

"I am crucified with Christ: nevertheless I live; yet not I, but
Christ liveth in me: and the life which I now live in the flesh
I live by the faith of the Son of God, who loved me, and gave
himself for me."

— GALATIANS 2:20 KJV

The third foundational principle of this B.E.S.T. life is "Body Dead." I really struggle with the negativity of this statement because I like alive, quickened, and positive affirmations of this faith walk. I could not escape the simplicity of this war/battle going on between the spirit and the flesh (sarx.) John quotes Jesus as saying, "The flesh profits nothing but the words that I speak to you, they are spirit and they are life," (John 6:63.) The earth suit we live in is made in the image of God and we are beautiful creatures. We are bought with a price and God loved us so much that He gave His only Son so we could be saved rather than condemned. Galatians 2:20 in the King James Version of the Bible gives the apostle Paul's description of a life that is not his own. He articulates a life that implies a crucifixion which requires the end result of death. Paul also teaches us that "for me to live is Christ, to die is gain" and "to be absent from the body is to be present with the Lord." I believe it is important we recognize that we have a special treasure in our earthen vessel. God no longer writes his laws on tablets of stones, but on the tablets of our hearts, according to 2 Corinthians 3:3. We are to be living letters that show forth the glory of our Creator by being doers of His Word in our expressions on earth.

We have this treasure in earthen vessels.

> *"But we have this treasure in earthen vessels, that the excellency of the power may be of God, and not of us. We are troubled on every side, yet not distressed; we are perplexed, but not in despair; Persecuted, but not forsaken; cast down, but not destroyed. Always bearing about in the body the dying of the Lord Jesus, that the life also of Jesus might be made manifest in our body. For we which live are alway delivered unto death for Jesus' sake, that the life also of Jesus might be made manifest in our mortal flesh. So then death worketh in us, but life in you."*

— 2 CORINTHIANS 4:7-12 KJV

What an awesome privilege and responsibility. We are responsible for housing the glory that is the life of God in us and we are to integrate Spirit, Soul, and Body into oneness with His purposes (Father, Son, and Holy Spirit.) Just as the Father, Son, and Holy Spirit are three in one, so are we to be three in one. This unity requires that He increase, we decrease or die. We are to put off the works of darkness and the evil desires of our own self-destruction so we can put on the nature that brings life. Just like the death of a seed produces multiple opportunities for future life, the death of our own fleshly desires and willful submission through the renewing of our mind or being soul fed will enable us to produce life in our "earthen vessel." We are a spiritual being, we have a soul that guides the willful choices of our life and we live in an earth suit that houses our spirit. This body of flesh is wicked and evil except when it dies to self and lives unto the One who made it.

Many have heard the story of dry bones in Ezekiel. Below is a passage from this story where Ezekiel is told to "prophesy" or speak the word of the Lord to these dry bones.

> *"Again he said unto me, Prophesy upon these bones, and say unto them, O ye dry bones, hear the word of the LORD. Thus saith the Lord GOD unto these bones; Behold, I will cause breath to enter into you, and ye shall live: And I will lay sinews upon you, and will bring up flesh upon you, and cover you with skin, and put breath in you, and ye shall live; and ye shall know that I am the LORD."*

— EZEKIEL 37: 4-6 KJV

Our God is able to supply all we need to make dry bones live again. He is able to provide the breath/pneuma/spirit along with the tissue or sinew needed to cause bones to be useful again. Our flesh profits nothing until it comes in contact with the purposeful breath of the Holy Spirit and His purposes for our life. These purposes are clearly articulated throughout His Word, but we often give attention to so many other observable earthly voices and phenomena. Being dead in our body is not hopeless and we do not miss out. When we submit our pleasures, desires, and wants to His purposes, He is able to impact our dry bones with new life from His breath and He will cause our dry bones to live again. The same spirit that raised Jesus from the tomb is able to quicken or make alive your mortal body (Romans 8:11.) The Word of God is life to us when we find them and health to all our flesh (Proverbs 4: 22.) "Body Dead" is representative of our submission and crucifixion of our own evil desires so we can walk in the law of the spirit of life instead of the law of sin and death. Death has no more victory over a Child of God who receives the promise of the Spirit through faith.

It is interesting that the word submission has so much negativity in our world today. Humility and submission are terms many consider to be weak; however, nothing could be further from the truth. Both terms represent a gateway into greatness. Throughout the Bible, humility is considered a prerequisite to honor and elevated success. Submission to the right governing authority is a prerequisite to receiving authority of your own. "Body Dead" is an act of your willful choice to discipline yourself and allow your spirit and soul to rule over the evil dictates of the flesh. The spirit of man is the candle of the Lord and is in a constant battle with the evil desires of the flesh, but the victory is won by submitting to the will of God and crucifying the evil desires of the flesh while counting on the blood from Christ's sacrifice on the cross to cleanse us from all of our messed up choices. Spirit led people truly experience life that is through the gracious gift of faith God gives. Spirit led people choose to renew their mind or feed their soul so this renewal produces obedience to the commands of God and demonstrates a love reciprocated impacting the thoughts, words, and actions that are expressed in a body that may live to crave worldly pleasures or lusts. Soul feeding is the only way to transfer the grace of life from the spiritual domain into the daily walk of living on earth. In the Lord's Prayer, remember the desire is that God's will be done in earth as it is in heaven. We were given the right and responsibility to be ambassadors in earth and to use the earth of our body, that is crucified with Him, to experience a newness of life that walks in love, joy, peace, long-suffering, gentleness, meekness, goodness, faith, and temperance (Galatians 2:23.) Spirit led or walking in the spirit should cause us to reflect the fruit of the spirit. There is no law against living a life producing this kind of fruit. Being Spirit Led, Soul Fed, and Body Dead should cause us to be prepared for a life that is not just looking forward to heaven, but is ready to bring heaven to earth through the life He provides. Our flesh wants to rule. Crucify it. Our spirit wants to lead. Feed it.

> *"There is therefore now no condemnation to them which are in Christ Jesus, who walk not after the flesh, but after the Spirit. For the law of the Spirit of life in Christ Jesus hath made me free from the law of sin and death. For what the law could not do, in that it was weak through the flesh, God sending his own Son in the likeness of sinful flesh, and for sin, condemned sin in the flesh: That the righteousness of the law might be fulfilled in us, who walk not after the flesh, but after the Spirit,"*
>
> — ROMANS 8:1-4 KJV

B.E.S.T. LIFE AHEAD!

> *"The LORD says, "I will guide you along the best pathway for your life. I will advise you and watch over you."*
>
> — PSALMS 32:8 NLT

> *"The thief cometh not, but for to steal, and to kill, and to destroy: I am come that they might have life, and that they might have it more abundantly."*
>
> — JOHN 10:10 KJV

> *"So you should earnestly desire the most helpful gifts. But now let me show you a way of life that is best of all,"*
>
> — 1 CORINTHIANS 12:31 NLT

When we have learned to execute the prioritization of Spirit Led,

Soul Fed, and Body Dead, we are ready to experience our best life. I often pray for people who have experienced great loss or major transition with this principle of "your best days are ahead." We often look at our circumstances or challenges and lose sight of hope. Hope is an earnest expectation for good. The idea of your best days being ahead embraces hope. Hope is always good. Faith is the substance of things hoped for in life. Without hope, our lives descend into despair and the energy we need to conquer dwindles. I am confident that we can all face our life's challenges with the hope of our B.E.S.T. life ahead. The acronym for best represents principles that, if acted upon, will produce good fruits toward that end.

Your best life requires that you become yourself to benefit others, engage with and execute consistently on mission, strategically steward your gifts and talents, while living a life that is trustworthy.

- B - is for becoming.
- E - is for executing.
- S - is for strategic stewardship.
- T - is for trustworthy.

Your best life awaits by starting with the realization that leadership starts with you. Jesus' two commandments summarizing the whole law says to love God with all of your heart, soul, mind, and strength and love your neighbor as you do yourself. Your best life starts with your recognition that you are "fearfully and wonderfully made" (Psalms 134: 14 KJV) and your Heavenly Father is totally behind you. You have a purpose and destiny to reign over the struggles and challenges that try to distract you from your mission.

Championships are exciting and definitely special, but consider the journey. I get so frustrated with the flippant nature with which we celebrate a championship ring or trophy as the pinnacle of success. The Buffalo Bills were a team in the early 1990's that were among the elite teams in the decade; however, they were chided and ridiculed for not winning a championship four consecutive trips to the Super Bowl in 1990, 1991, 1992, and 1993. These losses must be super disappointing and a stain in the organizational history, but I'll bet players like

Thurmon Thomas and Bruce Smith are proud of what they accomplished in their years as a Bill. The Bills were still champions, even though they were never Super Bowl Champions. A franchise that could make it to four Super Bowls in a row must have been something special. I find we often push through life with such relentless effort and stress that we sometimes fail to slow down and give focus to who we want to become in the pursuit. Who I am is much more important than what I do, but what I do will improve if who I am wins.

Dr. Myles Munroe was the first leader I heard define leadership as "becoming yourself so you may benefit others." When your life is focused inward with response, and outward with ability, you have a real chance to be a complete human. Focus inward on growth and development where you align your virtues and values with His truth. Direct your outward expressions of service toward others so your impact is not selfish but an expression of love. I've often heard others say that "love is a verb." This popular saying has a premise that I believe to be worthy; however, I believe love is a person. We are told in 1 John that God is love. We learn in the gospel of John that there is "no greater love than this" (John 15: 13 KJV) that a man lay down his life for his friends. Jesus' leadership model was one of servanthood. He washed His disciples feet. He fed thousands on two occasions out of compassion for their needs. He humbled himself to commit the ultimate sacrifice on a cross and experienced the excruciating separation for the sins of the whole world. Paul tells us in Philippians to "let this mind be in you" (Philippians 2:5 KJV.) We are not God. We are not able or required to make the same sacrifices. We are required to be a living sacrifice transforming our thinking; we can be salt in an unsavory world and light in a dark place. Becoming yours true self will keep you on point and will earn the trust of others because your motivation to meet their needs demonstrates love. Becoming yourself so you can be what you need or your brother is far more motivating than becoming yourself for a trophy or a reward. Becoming your true self to benefit others is perpetual because the best version of yourself is needed in the multiple roles you serve in society. For me, my multiple roles as a teammate, husband, father, school leader, church leader, and friend all carry different responsibilities, but they require the selfless fruit of love. Love never fails, never gives up, and never seeks its own. Your best life starts with loving yourself and others enough to strive to become who you are supposed to be.

The second letter in "B.E.S.T." represents the word executing. Executing means carrying out or doing what you intend. How often do we set goals and make plans only to see them fade into "good intentions?" Intentions are only good when they are turned into actions. Executing around your mission and engaging on what matters most with intentional focus is the essence of this second principle. By becoming yourself, you will yield results through the execution of your life's important roles and goals. The law of the harvest teaches us we reap what we sow. If we sow diligent efforts toward desired outcomes where execution becomes a specific focus, not just a wish or hope, we will see results. We already looked at the scripture in James that taught us how we must be doers or executioners of the word we learn, not hearers only.

There used to be a commercial on tv that would run saying, "Knowledge is power." Knowledge means you know something, but there is a lot of knowledge that goes unused and causes fleeting success. Knowledge without execution is useless. We should strive to gain knowledge, understanding, and wisdom; however, we will not see movement or fruits of effectiveness without execution. Execution requires focused intent, focused action, and focused evaluation/scorekeeping. Later in this writing, I present a continuous improvement model of "FIX IT" communicating a process for growth and change that speaks to this cycle of focus, investment, and examination. Failure is rarely final or fatal. Most times, when we execute on a mission, we get opportunities to adjust to changes in the environment while we are doing the work. Your best life is ahead if you have the integrity to take a stand and decide that executing your mission matters to you. Benjamin Franklin said, "Well done is better than well said." Talk is cheap, right? Let the results of your execution do the talking.

The "S" in BEST is definitely packed with fruit producing potential. Strategic stewardship means one uses his/her gifts, talents, abilities, and resources in concert with the intended outcomes. Strategy is the game plan which maps your course of execution. Stewardship is the taking of responsibility for what you possess. Strategic stewardship is found in the articulation of LIVE LIFE LOUD. The Gospel of Luke gives us the most complete account of Jesus' teaching on faithfulness. In this passage, Jesus is teaching on three areas of faithfulness that lead to greater levels of responsibility. He requires us to be faithful in the little things, that which is another man's, and unrighteous mammon (material things.) When we prove to be faithful in the little things, we graduate to bigger things. When we are faithful with that which is another man's, we are able to obtain that which is our own. When we prove faithful with worldly goods and material things, we graduate to true kingdom riches.

> *"He that is faithful in that which is least is faithful also in much: and he that is unjust in the least is unjust also in much. If therefore ye have not been faithful in the unrighteous mammon, who will commit to your trust the true riches? And if ye have not been faithful in that which is another man's, who shall give you that which is your own? No servant can serve two masters: for either he will hate the one, and love the other; or else he will hold to the one, and despise the other. Ye cannot serve God and mammon. Luke 16:10-13 KJV The apostle Paul writes to the Corinthian church in their first letter from him that, "moreover it is required in stewards, that a man be found faithful."*

> — I CORINTHIANS 4:2 KJV

This word faithful means trustworthy and dependable. We are expected to be dependable and just in the little things, with money and possessions, and with other people's resources. Strategic stewardship requires we love God more than money, we take care of the little things, and we give attention to those things that are others' as well as our own. I think it is important to note that climbing the ladder of success requires the faithfulness to be good and do good to those who help you along the way. We climb the ladder of success on the backs of other good men/women, but we shouldn't step on their faces in our zeal to climb. Strategic stewardship is being disciplined to care for the little things in preparation for the bigger things coming. Your best life is created by doing the little things well and taking care to rule over your money and possessions rather than letting them rule you.

It is often quoted, "²Trust is the currency of leadership." I'm not sure who the author of the quote is; however, there is an article with this title in Forbes magazine. In this magazine, the author, Rajeev Peshawaria, tells of a survey done on the most trusted people in the lives of executives and they are usually mother (first), father (second), and a close friend (third.) If we desire to lead ourselves and others well, we need trust. The law of the harvest comes into focus again. If you want to build trust, you must first be trustworthy. The last key attribute or principle to living your best life is being "trustworthy." We do not have control over the level of trust in an organization with many other individuals, but we do have control over our level of trustworthiness or faithfulness. One key way to build trust is to make and keep commitments. Be careful promising things that you can't deliver. As a young leader, one of the greatest challenges was determining between the work in which I should personally invest versus the work better served through delegation. The balance in this decision-making is critical. Delegate too much and you are just lazy and/or disinterested. Delegate too little and you are just autocratic and controlling. When considering the word trustworthy, some other words come to mind: integrity, honesty, authenticity, and transparency. I've worked in places where the real vision, mission, and beliefs were vague as well as the focus of our work. The transparency was not there and the cliche phrases lose power because there is no integrity of action meeting intent. The easiest way to improve levels of trust in an organization is to simplify the commitments. Make those commitments solid, and then execute around them until they are no longer relevant or there is a greater need.

Every year during natural breaks in my calendar, I take time and pull up a document that has a heading for Spirit, Heart, Mind, Body. Under each heading, I type two or three commitments I will make for growth in that area of my life. I usually set a goal under "Spirit" related to the

Bible and other books that feed my knowledge for the Creator. I also establish daily commitments to execute my own personal quiet time for study, reflection, meditation and journaling. The heading "Heart" includes commitments to the key people in my life. Currently, for the last three years, the commitment has been to be a better listener by setting up critical communication junctures in my life such as family meetings, spouse one-on- one time, and relationship time with my closest friends and/or mentors and mentees. For example, Amy and I intentionally share one thing we are thankful for related to the actions of the other. The heading of "Mind" involves commitments to reading certain books for personal and professional growth and even commitments to journaling so I am able to keep my communication skills moving in a positive direction. The "Body" section has two subsections that relate to endurance and strength. It should probably have a third subset of diet, but that's still something I've not had the courage to take on personally. In the endurance subsection, I set a goal for endurance running usually like the Duncan Ridge 50K or the Georgia Jewel 50 miler. In the strength subsection, I usually set goals around timed completion of push ups, pull ups or unique workouts like Murph (1 mile run, 100 pull ups, 200 push ups, 300 air squats, 1 mile run.) These commitments are typed and revisited twice a year. September and June are the times I revisit these goal sheets. The daily commitments required to make these things happen are inspiring and help me remember what and who I value, prioritizing my work accordingly. Being trustworthy is an honorable trait that can be sharpened or improved in life's furnaces of adversity. Staying true to yourself and walking in integrity is much easier when there is a practice of "daily private victories" that feeds the furnace of your internal drive to succeed. I encourage you to develop a daily routine of reflection and journaling helps you sustain a focus on priorities driving your life in a way that matters. If you want to lead people who matter to do things that matter, you have to know what matters and execute around them. That builds trust.

Your B.E.S.T. life is ahead. All it takes to get better is to do better. All it takes to do better is to do a little more than you did yesterday. Becoming the best version of you matters. We need you. There is no one like you, so be your unique you. Executing creates movement that helps you stay on the path of improvement. Figure out a focus that matters to you and execute around that focus or mission. Strategically steward the gifts, talents, abilities, and resources that are available. As you are faithful and dependable with the little things in your hands now, you grow your potential to steward more in life. Build the capacity to be trusted by first trusting God. Trust His principles and determine you will make and keep commitments to yourself and others that promote His best in your life.

> *"Trust in the Lord with all thine heart; and lean not unto thine own understanding. In all thy ways, acknowledge Him and He shall direct thy paths."*
>
> — PROVERBS 3:5-6 KJV

10

"FIX IT" MINDSET: PERSONAL & ORGANIZATIONAL CONTINUOUS IMPROVEMENT

C arol Dweck wrote a popular book called *Mindset: The New Psychology of Success: How We Can Learn to Fulfill Our Potential*. The book talks about the growth mindset versus a fixed mindset. There has been much research and work done on brain development in all age groups as well as in brain recovery. This concept of growth mindset is not just a psychological principle of growth, but it is also a physiological reality. My father recently had a stroke leaving him paralyzed on his right side. Through research, the doctors know the stroke caused by a blockage in his brains' blood vessels on his left side impacted multiple functions of his thought processes as well as physiological responses of movement on his right side. Using a variety of speech therapies, occupational therapies, and physical therapies, recovery of previously lost functions have gradually happened. We have learned the brain that is damaged can repair itself, sometimes regenerate some tissue, and often reroute messages so a part of the brain function that is lost can be trained to be compensated for.

The most important fact I learned in assisting dad with much of his therapy is that the number one thing impacting a patient's recovery is activity. You cannot sit and wait for things to therapeutically return without effort and effort is hard to come by if there is no hope and expectation that growth can occur. The level of difficulty of recovery for an older stroke patient is often much higher because of the speed of muscular atrophy and the rapid descent of belief in a mind that is so used to the automaticity of functions lost in the impacting event. Carol Dweck addresses in her book the importance of mindset and how a growth mindset truly impacts the outcomes when compared to a fixed mindset.

What is a growth mindset? Growth mindset is the mindset that believes "I can get better, stronger, faster, smarter." Fixed mindset is usually the entrenching belief that "it is what it is" or "That's just the way I am." As a math teacher, it would be impossible for me to count how many times parents and students alike have made the comment, "I can't do math because it's not my thing." The reality is some people may have a proclivity toward higher functioning in some domains of learning, but research suggests we can all get better and increase our capabilities in nearly any field of endeavor we apply ourselves to. Growth does not necessarily bring the promise of success or victory, but growth implies I can improve and get better. This mindset is important for us to recognize with this section of the book. I believe one of the most critical components of effective growth and accomplishment of potential is this idea that I can apply myself to anything and get better. It then behooves me to identify what matters to me and prioritize the work around what I feel is going to most impact my success. This acronym of "FIX IT" could be called a mindset and process simultaneously. Consider the fixed mindset that says, "it is what it is; so I can't change it." That is a losing mentality that entraps us in mediocrity; however, a "FIX IT" mindset says "I can apply myself or we can apply ourselves to creative cooperation in ways that integrate all our our best talents and resources toward improvement." Continuous improvement ought to be desired personally and professionally in any individual and/or organization. The fundamental components of movement in a positive direction toward improvement can be found in a few simple principles that are actionable. It all starts with a belief that we can grow and "fix it."

As an educational administrator, one part of my daily responsibilities is to facilitate a healthy discipline plan with policies that are equitable and fair. The first step in any process requiring the administration of discipline is to investigate and identify the action that needs correction and how that correction can be best carried out. Obviously, the more the person who committed an offense can identify his/her own mistake or misdeed that has run afoul of expectations, the more likely a successful intervention will be employable. The first thing I try to do when investigating is identify the what. What is the offense? Next, I usually try to identify the "why." There are a variety of consequences that may be assigned to deter or discourage the offender from participating in the same behavior in the future; however, there is no greater deterrent to bad behavior than a desire in the individual to no longer participate in such behavior. I really try hard to have another person own his/her misbehavior(s) before I try to assign some consequence. Many times the offense is surprising, simple, and swift. In such cases where a person makes a bad choice that does not warrant a full blown "due process" hearing with witnesses and statements, I simply identify what appeared to be the issue and ask the student, "Can you fix it?" If they own it and agree to fix it, I move on as do they. The idea of fixing it requires that we know the "it" and we know a way to do or not do it again. I tend to be a "to the point" individual. My role as father is one I cherish and I love my kids. I expect them to act consistently with integrity around our established family values and norms. When one of them does something inconsistent with those expectations, I am often able to use the phrase "fix it" and they know what I mean. The responsibility is on them to identify the problem, solve it, and make sure it stays solved so significant weight in consequences don't have to follow.

I used the analogy of discipline in the home and schools to illustrate the essence of the "fix it" mentality because there are some parallels consistent with any improvement process and the improvement of meeting expectations where behavior is concerned. First, there is a reason something needs to be fixed. Some behavior has collided with what is expected whether the act was committed intentionally or accidentally. The second major analogous reality is the act has already been done and we can no longer change it. We can assess the cause, the damage, the why, but we can't change that something happened. Our power is now in the reality that we can learn from the mistake and make adjustments. The more we dwell on the misdeed and the foul nature of the incident itself, the less we are able to move forward; however, there has to be a confronting of the brutal facts and responsibility taken so there is a clear understanding of expectations moving forward. The framework of "fix it" was birthed out of wanting to simplify the process of improvement without trivializing the important work that has to be done for an individual or institution to accomplish greater success. F.I.X. I.T. stands for focus, invest, x-ray, integrity, trust. The next few sections will expand on what each of these terms in this acronym of "FIX IT" stands for and why they contribute to a more complete process of improvement.

FOCUS

F.I.X. I.T. starts with focus. Focus or fix your eyes/mind/thoughts on principles and the desired outcomes of your life that align with them. Consider the 3 P's - Principles, Purpose, Passion. Personal improvement starts first with knowing the principles you will value and give attention to, the purpose of your existence, and the passion that motivates you to do what you do. Focus is a simple way of thinking about looking under a microscope to see who, what, when, where, how, and why. Everything we deal with in life matters, but we can't focus on everything at once. Pinpointing the need for a focus or a target of our efforts for improvement requires deep thought and real brutal honesty. Vision, mission, and beliefs should be an overarching contributor to the focus of our work. For instance, my personal mission statement is to lead people who matter to do things that matter. This statement gives my life focus and allows me to remind myself that I value leadership, I value people, and I value doing stuff that matters. Sometimes my focus may be on the people at work. Sometimes my focus is on the people at home. Sometimes my focus is on the people in my local church. Sometimes my focus is on my extended family. Sometimes my focus is on the stranger walking down the side of the road with no ride to work. If you've never considered evaluating your personal vision, mission, and beliefs, I would like to encourage you to consider doing so. Giving thought to the desired outcomes of your life and what your life will focus on and who you want to become is fundamental to a life lived on purpose. Consider identifying the principles that stand out as core beliefs in how you plan to do the work of your life. Consider your purpose by considering other great leaders or heroes in your life that have impacted you deeply. What are your favorite quotes and scriptures? Develop a set of ideas or statements that can serve as the foundational work of a simplified mission statement. Remember to consistently consider any inputs from mission, vision, and beliefs of an organization or individual you are working with so there is alignment within what you choose to "FIX."

FIX IT needs to be employed to evaluate what the facts of your situation are that cry out for improvement. When I gave my example in the opening paragraph about leading people who matter to do things that matter, I consider it important to establish focus in each role of my life. Major areas of focus for me are my roles as a spouse, father, school leader, church leader, and runner. I only draw a paycheck in one of those roles, but they are all important to me. I set a focus (often the outcome is a goal) that ensures intentionality and value is added to that role in my life. This work of setting the focus allows me to have some level of impact on my circumstances because I work to create some intentionality in the workspace. Focus in organizations and individual lives often shift due to imbalances in areas that require adjustments. The first expression of the "fix it" mindset is to identify the focus, the Big Hairy Audacious Goal, the WIG (Wildly Important Goal), a desired outcome. Identify what matters and the factors that impact the matter the most. In school improvement planning, this starts each year for me revisiting all of the data and metrics that matter to us as a school. We look at a variety of data. Of course, test scores make up a big portion of our data review, but we have perception data through staff, parent, and student surveys. We have reviews that require us to connect the dots between expenditures and areas of focus and its impact on the test scores. We look at data in a variety of subgroups to assess equity. We are often so data rich or data saturated that it can be hard to really do an appropriate "needs assessment" and identify a focus big enough to impact the work of all while being focused enough to keep our attention. This portion of "FIX IT" is often where difficult conversations about the current reality are birthed. This portion should include a real "gut check" and heart check up causing you to look deeply at who you are and who you want to be...what you do and what you want to do better...what you are for and what you are not for...etc.

In education, we utilize "SMART" goals. SMART is an acronym that helps us identify what is required in setting a good goal.

- S - means it is specific enough that you know exactly what you are measuring and how it will be communicated.
- M-means measurable. SMART goals have to articulate a specific measure that can be given a value.
- A-means attainable or actionable. We want to set goals that are realistically attainable. We also want to make sure we can actually do something about.
- R-means relevant. A good goal has to be worthy of the work and relevant to what matters to you or your organization.
- Time-bound or timely means there is a what by when.

All areas of focus may not require a SMART goal or a measurable outcome, but the most effective way to improve is to take advantage of lead measures believed to impact the bigger focus. In school, our SMART goal may be based on the Georgia Milestones Reading Assessment and we may establish a percentage increase we hope to see, but we may also set some goals throughout the year using assessments we have in the building that measure Lexile so we can evaluate students for readiness prior to the summative assessment at the end. In businesses, there are financial reports reviewed regularly to see if sales are hitting projections or if performance is hitting the target. One shoe business I read about reviewed data and determined that a person is 90% more likely to buy a shoe if they try on more than one pair of shoes. As a result of this information, they decided to track an additional "lead measure" to assist them with hitting their monthly target for sales. They started measuring the number of times sales associates were able to coax folks into trying on more than 1 pair of shoes. The incentives became tied to this lead measure. Consider the power of this in a culture like a shoe store. Sales associates are probably naturally incentivized to be warm and inviting and create a friendly atmosphere for customers because they are being rewarded for how many shoes they are able to get people to try on rather than how many they can sell. Hopefully, as we set a focus on the right measures that matter, we stumble upon many strategies that help us improve far more than one metric. The F - in FIX it stands for focus. That focus can be a "SMART" goal or a much less complicated set of standards for targeting strategies toward improvement. Personally, I set running goals for a longer event like the Georgia Jewel 50 miler. That goal then drives me to consider other targets I need to set for myself to make that possible such as improved diet, better hiking, and equipment purchase. The most important thing about this first phase is that the focus is clearly defined in terms of outcomes and expectations. You develop the action steps and/or strategies that will be necessary to carry out the plan.

INVEST

Once you have decided on your focus and you know where you are putting some intentional effort toward improvement, it is time to consider all that must be integrated to INVEST appropriately in the right outcomes. In this phase, we integrate thoughts, actions, and cooperatives to carry out the principle-centered goal, mission, or aim of our desired outcomes. Take actions consistent with your focus. Consider an "entertainment system" and the integration of multiple components to enhance what used to just be watching T.V. One component can get out of sync and the whole system is compromised. Investing in the work or executing around the focus of your desired outcomes is the real test of integrity. Can you act in ways that "put your money where your mouth is?" Does the energy, effort, financial resources, and human resources aim effectively at what we said our focus was?

In schools, this phase is the most difficult and longest phase. Focus without investment is frustrating. I have been a part of many teams where we had such excitement around a goal or project and we knew where we planned to focus our energy, but in the daily grind, we somehow lost track of what we said we would do. People on the team have to know what their investments will be and how we will hold one another accountable in positive ways to encourage the growth necessary to see the growth desired. You can't "fake it 'til you make it" because you'll never "FIX IT" without intentionally investing in strategic action that is able to be monitored, celebrated, and adjusted. A great resource for improving this portion of your improvement game is The 4 Disciplines of Execution: Achieving Your Wildly Important Goals. To take a deeper look at how business can really apply four disciplines to ensure execution occurs, this is a worthy read. I would just like to keep this process as simple as possible. Invest in the right actions and strategies, find the right "lead measures" to establish and maintain accountability, write and report on important inputs and outputs regularly. In my own personal life, if I set a goal to run an ultra-marathon (anything over 26.2 is considered an ultra-marathon) I have certain actions and strategies I take including mileage goals per week, cross training maintenance goals, and some diet goals. I hold myself accountable through writing out the plan, re-writing the plan as it changes, and keeping a log of the results of each of the actions I take. The investment stage is where you do the work, relate to all the players, and evaluate the information you have that confirms or denies success. Don't wait on making adjustments. As soon as you are missing targets, determine whether or not the targets were unreasonable to begin with or if you are just in need of better investments. Once you've decided what you'll do, invest. The process of carrying the strategies and actions out may immediately begin to yield observable results letting you know of adjustments you need to make. This phase often bleeds into the third phase of "FIX IT," which is X-ray or examine. The moment data is ready to review, you should be reviewing it. For my runs, I constantly think about what went well with the run and what did not. Did my hydration work out or do I need a better plan or better tool? Are there nagging injuries I can identify the cause of? I don't have to wait until I'm done executing the plan to see problems and adjust.

X-RAY OR EXAMINE

Be ready, be real, and be responsive. What does an X-Ray do? It looks into a body of tissue at very specific details of how things should look so health professionals can identify what is normal vs. what is abnormal. As we examine our investments toward our desired outcome, we determine what needs to be celebrated and what needs to be improved upon. As you look into the reality of where you are and what results your investments are yielding, you must be ready to be on the lookout for what's going well and what is not. You must also be real or "confront the brutal facts" so you don't hide from the truth of your current reality. Lastly, you have to be responsive. You can't be willing to just do the same old thing as you discover it's not working.

I think one of my greatest struggles during this final phase of "FIX IT" is celebrating. If you are working with a team, how will that team know they are moving in the right direction and making a difference if we do not articulate that through a celebration? Celebrations are not always elaborate and costly. Most of the time a simple pat on the back or a word of encouragement is as valuable as a medal around one's neck. Praise when things are praiseworthy. Simple expressions of praise encourage repeat behaviors and are often the simplest and most responsive approaches to replicating good outcomes.

Unfortunately, praise is not always the result of our examination of the progress toward our desired outcomes. Sometimes there are barriers that need to be discussed and roadblocks that have to be removed. When you bump up against negative data that gives you a picture of negative results, be careful not to degenerate or cast down your team, but be real. Use this phase of "FIX IT" to build team trust, authenticity, and growth. Try to infuse meaningful data snapshots that point to the truth of what you need to see in order to evaluate growth. As a leader, I find it is important for me to step away from the data and solutions and listen to my team first because once I go down a certain path, they are all just following. The people doing the work know better about what adjustments in the work need to be made in order for that work to hit the target.

INTEGRITY

To have meaningful conversations that celebrate the good and adjust for the bad, integrity and trust must both be present. Integrity, in this sense, is all about being honest and evaluating with transparency the alignment of our mission, actions, strategies, results, and culture. If you do a great job, get bonuses, but you obtained them with a lack of integrity like some school districts where teachers and administrators cheated on the standardized tests you lack integrity. Integrity requires the work we do can be talked about with honor because of how we do it and because of the results the work is getting. We can also face the facts if our work is not yielding what we want, even if it disappoints or hurts our feelings. If any part of our team is not fully integrated and fully invested, our integrity as a team will suffer.

TRUST

Trust has a significant impact on speed of action and the ability of an organization to be nimble. General Stanley McChrystal wrote *Team of Teams: New Rules of Engagement for a Complex World*. One "take away" I got from reading General McChrystal was that we must be nimble or able to adjust quickly on the fly. We are faced with great complexity in the multiple systems operating in our world. General McChrystal articulates in this book that the battlefield looked so different in the streets of a post-Saddam Iraq and in the turmoil created by the war in Afghanistan that our Special Operations Forces were forced to adapt and become more nimble. One major building block to speeding up operations and responding to threats was to build more trust and simplify a system to speed up communication for operations that would typically take longer to plan and get approved. If a target of opportunity presents itself, structures have to be changed and simplified to allow the boots on the ground to make more decisions and get less feedback up the chain of command in order to increase this nimbleness. In this acronym of "FIX IT," trust is the caboose on the train, but it is not the last component. The entire process of focusing, investing, and examining requires integrity and trust throughout the operation or the work will spring a leak. One thing to keep in mind as you promote trust on your team is that, in order to promote trust, complexity has to be simplified, transparency has to be normalized, and respect (love and value) has to be amplified.

Whatever mission or challenge is before you, you can FIX IT. You can identify a meaningful focus and clearly articulate a desired outcome with confidence. You can invest in the right opportunities for growth and change while integrating your resources in ways that connect the dots. You can eXamine your progress and results consistently to establish the checkpoints of meaningful celebration and critical adjustments. You can build integrity in your team and promote trust so the cycle will continue to produce and reproduce fruit of growth and positive change. If it matters to you, you can FIX IT.

IV

DISCIPLESHIP AND
DEVOTIONALS

Prior to the "daily devotional" section of the book, I want to submit some short articles whose purpose is to remind us of discipleship principles we continuously need. R.P.M. reminds us of our daily responsibility to grow self in relation to our knowledge of God. I challenge you to do a search of the scriptures for the phrase "knowledge of God" and see what you find. We grow in wisdom and understanding as we grow in the knowledge of God, and we cannot apply in our lives without reading, meditating, and praying in accordance with all that is written. Jesus passed the test with "it is written." We can too.

Following R.P.M. is a very practical article on the 3 D's. With R.P.M., we delve into the spiritual feeding of ourselves for daily life while the reminders of the 3 D's give us some intentional areas of focused discipleship for meaningful execution. One of the key values of most successful people is hard work. A more complete definition of that is diligence. Read the article and work to incorporate the R.P.M. of read, pray, and meditate and the D's of decisive, disciplined, and diligence into your leadership repertoire. You will increase the chances of championship execution of this life as a disciple of Christ.

"Spring Cleaning" gives us a parable that relates to our life with some practical insights about the importance of taking responsibility for conducting the spring cleaning in our lives. "Life is Like Growing Tobacco" is an article that connects lessons I learned throughout my years of working with my father, grandfather, and uncle on a tobacco farm. There are no greater examples to spiritual reality than those found in the natural laws of life on a farm. Hope these two practical articles are able to be just that, practical.

Following these first two articles, you will find daily devotionals that should be long enough to feed your desire for growth and provide meaningful reminders. These devotionals are written with a quote, scriptures from the Word of God, a written focus from the aforementioned, and a prayer of execution. Housed in each prayer is a combination of scriptural commitments, positive affirmations, and confirming adoration for the character of the One to whom we pray. I hope that these devotionals teach, encourage, remind, and inspire you to develop the Heart of a Champion while you LIVE LIFE LOUD. May they feed your soul as you seek to be SPIRIT LED, SOUL FED, BODY DEAD as you pursue the B.E.S.T. Life Ahead. May God bless you richly with all wisdom and power to live your life in alignment with the Holy Spirit's direction while walking the grace purchased by the Son's blood, as you rest in the confidence that comes from the constant expression of our Father's love.

RPM = READ, PRAY, MEDITATE

I like to talk in acronyms that help me remember key principles or thoughts that are critical for execution. This RPM acronym comes from the idea of a dragstrip. I have often watched some of the television shows such as "Pinks" and "Outlaw" where people race cars for pink slips or money. These short events require each race begin with the motor getting revved up to obtain maximum RPMs so the car can appropriately use its horsepower at the starting line and throughout the quarter mile run. In the Christian life, I believe starting the day with a moment of RPM will get your spiritual engine revved up for the run throughout the day. You cannot rely on an old burnout or the tuning of a week ago (last Sunday's message) to prepare you for the race you run today. The components of RPM are simple and probably obvious. Read the Word of God. All scripture is inspired by God to provide us with the instruction, correction, and direction so we can be ready for our day. Throughout the Bible, we are told to keep His Word before our eyes, in our mouth, and in our hearts (see Proverbs 4:20-24, Joshua 1:8, & Psalms 119 KJV.) Read the Bible and read good commentaries, devotionals, and other encouraging texts that feed you Godly principles.

> *"After this manner therefore pray ye: Our Father which art in heaven, Hallowed be thy name. Thy kingdom come. Thy will be done in earth, as it is in heaven. Give us this day our daily bread. And forgive us our debts, as we forgive our debtors. And lead us not into temptation, but deliver us from evil: For thine is the kingdom, and the power, and the glory, for ever. Amen."*

> — MATTHEW 6:9-13 KJV

Next is "pray." Jesus taught us a prayer that takes less than a minute. We can use it as a guide. "Our Father who art in heaven, hallowed be thy name..." (Matthew 6: 9-13.) Worship God and acknowledge that He is God and His standards are what we hope to share in our daily lives. "Thy kingdom come, thy will be done in earth as it is in heaven..." God's kingdom is an important reality that is often overlooked. He has eternal kingdom purposes carried out by us, His representatives or ambassadors. This portion of the prayer is yielding the earthen vessel of ourselves in obedience to His purposes and plans. We are commissioned to bring heavenly purposes to earth through our obedience to truth. "Give us this day, our daily bread..." We can pray that God blesses us with what we need so we can feed this earth suit and to be servants who take care of His sheep. We can pray for the provision we need to accomplish His kingdom purposes. "Forgive our trespasses as we forgive those who trespass against us. Lead us not into temptation, but deliver us from evil." We must forgive. Forgiveness should come naturally. We never have to forgive to the degree our

Savior has forgiven us. If we don't forgive, He cannot forgive us because that is a natural/supernatural law. God doesn't lead us into temptation, He delivers us from evil and always provides the way to escape evil. Why do bad things happen to good people? Because there are no good people. We all earned bad from our bad, but He has redeemed us from the curse of the law which is, as follows: temptation leads to lust, lust (evil desire) leads to sin, sin leads to death. Thanks be to God we are free from the law of sin and death because of the law of the spirit of life in Christ Jesus.

The "M" is meditation. I think we often miss out on a powerful tool of connection between the Spirit of truth in the Word and the power of the mind in our earthen vessel. Joshua 1:8 teaches us to meditate on the book of the law (the Word) so we can observe to do according to what's in it. The promised result is we prosper and have good success. When we read, pray, and meditate on a consistent basis, we rev up the engine of our soul and prepare ourselves for running our race in a much more effective way.

Heavenly Father, you are God. You are the King of Kings and I desire to submit my life to your Kingdom purposes. Help me to comprehend in your Word the truth needed for me to execute my calling today. You promise that when I don't know how to pray as I should, Holy Spirit prays for me. Help the meditation of my heart and mind be on truth that enables me to serve You and Your people as I seek to bring heavenly influence to earth through obedience to your commands. In Christ's holy name I pray and believe that you are able to do exceedingly abundantly more than I have asked or prayed, Amen.

THE THREE D'S: WILL YOU BE DECISIVE, DISCIPLINED, AND DILIGENT?

These three words that begin with "d" have often been in my vocabulary about personal leadership and utilized in a variety of ways. This iteration comes from a morning drive when it was evident many of the folks I am surrounded by are facing challenges, fears, and struggles. I must admit I have often found myself in a similar battle and needing some of my own advice surrounding the 3 D's. 3D stands for three dimensional and is representative of looking at something that is lifelike. In this year of 2020, 3D fits nicely into our metaphorical language for clarity of sight. If we can implement these 3 D's into our daily habits, we will likely be effective and ensure a course that is not just a flat, 2D trajectory, but one that is full of texture and elevation. Consider "Google Earth" and the difference made when looking at a map of mountainous regions compared to a simpler 2D map. The images express so much more as contour seems to be revealed and the magnitude of elevation is easier to distinguish. In life, when we consistently live out these 3 D's meaning decisive, disciplined, and diligent, we will have access to a better map with better features helping us and those who we work with to find a better destination.

Be decisive. What precedes any action or outcome? A decision. You have the power to choose, thus you have the power of decisiveness. You can decide your attitude and action in every moment of every day. As long as we are not speaking about an automated response, our decisiveness is under our control and the results of those choices paint the canvas of our life in strokes that enrich or denigrate the picture. Decide what you want your outcomes to be. Begin with the end in mind and make room for focused priorities rather than embracing every new trend and opportunity. You decide when to say yes or no. Decide what values you hold as virtuous and what you will believe. You decide what roles you will play and the actions within those roles. You decide to schedule your priorities rather than prioritizing your schedule. Being decisive really comes from the basic roots of the first habit of *The 7 Habits of Highly Effective People* by Stephen R. Covey. Being proactive is the habit of personal responsibility and speaks to one's ability to "make their own weather." You choose your attitudes and actions. Decide what you want in the "end" and make decisions now that put you in a position to act right.

Be disciplined. Webster's online dictionary defines discipline as: control gained by enforcing obedience or order, b: orderly or prescribed conduct or pattern of behavior, c. SELF -CONTROL. Notice the words "control" and "self-control." Discipline is the root of effectiveness in leadership because leadership starts with self. Epiclettus said, "No man is free who is not a master of himself." Do you have control over yourself? Do you obey you? Is your life orderly and lived according to "prescribed" conduct or patterns of behavior that get you the results you want? Discipline usually results from great understanding of vision and purpose. It's much easier to discipline your body to prepare for something when you have an idea of what you are preparing for and you value the purpose of the pursuit. I do much better with my training and/or running when I have a goal (time or repetition accomplishment) or objective (race.) Living with direction necessitates having direction inside of yourself like a compass. Can you use your maps of decisiveness to set the bearing and travel in a direction with which you are content and moving toward your end? Discipline is all about patterns of behavior with predictable results. If you make important decisions but you are not sure what kind of actions and discipline will help you get there, start with breaking the goal down into smaller parts to win small battles consistently. Discipline or "bringing under control" is most void when dealing with destructive habits not good for us (alcohol abuse, drug abuse, tobacco abuse, etc.) Disciplined thought and disciplined action are important. How we think determines how we act; how we act becomes what people see. It all starts in the mind and how we think about important things in our lives.

Be diligent. Diligence is working hard at the right things in the right way consistently. Hard work is a key to success, but you can work hard at the wrong thing and get a wrong or unwanted result. Ensure we are working hard at the right things. It's pointless to slave away on something that is not really important to you. Taking pride in your work or deeply caring about the outcomes of your sweat equity is a valuable trait. I was always taught by my father and grandfather, "If it's worth doing, it's worth doing right." Diligence involves commitment, hard work, and exactitude. Are you committed to finish with a pace that demonstrates value? A quick search on Google yields "careful and persistent work or effort." Once you decide to do something and you demonstrate the discipline to commit, diligence ensures the quality of work is "careful and persistent."

Heavenly Father, may my life be committed to becoming the ambassador you expect me to be. Help me to demonstrate decisiveness, discipline, and diligence in all the work I undertake. Come Holy Spirit and reveal to me how to make good decisions and be disciplined to do what your Word says. Most importantly, help me to live like Enoch who had the testimony that he diligently sought after you. I commit to decisively follow your commands with discipline and diligence as I seek to obey. I thank you, Lord, that I pray with confidence because I know you are able to do exceedingly abundantly more than I could ask or think. In Christ's Holy name I pray, Amen.

11

LIFE APPLICATION: SPRING CLEANING

I t doesn't matter when it's done; spring cleaning is a process difficult to start but rewarding when complete. I find myself really dreading breaks when I know it is the time I set aside for "spring cleaning" in my office. I do it in spite of dread and dislike for the process because I know it brings order, occasional insight, and focus back into a fairly chaotic and busy space. My office is busy and often the "hot seat" of urgent and important interactions. I move from one situation to the next without the time (perhaps my own lack of discipline) to file away the last urgent matter or the peaceful demeanor to discern well what to discard and what to file. As I sit in my office and view stacks of different copies, documentation forms, personal notes about activities, incidents, meeting agendas, personnel letters, etc., I recognize the need to comb through the stack to decide what to file, discard, or shred. This process is potentially a beautiful metaphor for life. I simultaneously dread and peacefully anticipate this great event.

Here are some insights I think might apply to life and living:

It always looks worse before it looks better. Chadd Wright talks about how the coolest time of every day is right before dawn. As a Navy SEAL and ultra runner, he has done much of his most important work in the cover of darkness and has had to mentally sustain himself through the adversity of the darkest and coldest moments. According to Chadd, adversity gets to its peak level right before reaching a steady state or victory. The same is true of the silly desk disaster analogy. Amy and I were talking on the phone while I was cleaning (hands free, of course) and we discussed how, in the process of spring cleaning, these types of scenarios often look worse before they look better. Before I reap the fruit of a clear desktop, I unmask 3 months of hidden, neatly stowed stacks brought out into the open. Sometimes in life, we avoid peeling the scabs off the scars of humanity and actually deal with cleaning the wounds caused by our poor choices, negligent oversights, or uncontrollable circumstances. We deem it easier to tuck away and put aside until we are ready to deal efficiently with them. We have to "confront the [1]Brutal Facts" eventually and do some spring cleaning. Are their problems in the form of habits and mindsets that keep us cluttered and messy? Just like blowing out the carport, the stirring of dust is a necessary evil to achieve a clean space for living. What have we hidden in stacks that we avoid in our relationships, in our personal health, in our mental health, and our spiritual well-being?

Discernment and wisdom were needed to effectively categorize the stacks and cleaning of the mess. A variety of agendas I created, as well agendas from random meetings, were stacked under my desk, to the side of my desk, and on a table located against a side wall. There were old poster papers where important feedback from meetings were recorded. There were hand-written notes, legal documents, discipline testimonies, data files, etc. These items had a variety of destinations and each destination was important. I don't want to throw away important documentation that should be saved. I can't discard important personal information, and I may need to review some materials and remind myself of the purpose of the meetings. While going through these stacks or piles, I often come across meaningful documents that remind me of important information I forgot. Sometimes this information helps me to remember why we said we were doing a certain process or focusing in a certain area and it renews my commitment to make sure I am leading well in that area. I often find that I've overlooked some things that should have been done. Sometimes I find things to shred and know that shredding these documents means those days are behind and there is no benefit to living in the past because I have new information I can use moving forward to help us to set a new course. In this process, I need to be careful not to get careless and be in a hurry. I need to go through stacks carefully and not assume the extra copies of agendas are all the same form. I need to be able to identify where the stack shifts to another important document type.

One poster I found was of particular benefit and a great reminder of one of our School Improvement initiatives that was a "big rock." I took a picture before discarding so it could be remembered and documented in a way less cumbersome but readily available to "write the vision and make it plain," (Habakkuk 2:2 KJV.) In life, sometimes we run across great natural, self-evident truths we often file away and forget. It's important to take a personal inventory and find ways to use tools such as technology to save these insights for future use. Today, as I type this metaphorical insight, I am doing an inventory and creating my own brain map to the importance of "spring cleaning" in my own life. To treat the stacks appropriately, I need to be patient, take the time needed for review, and be diligent to do the right thing with the right documents so their future is saved or discarded appropriately. In your own daily life, do you evaluate mental files, experiences, and decisions to make space for creating meaningful checkpoints of reality helping you hold yourself accountable? I think a great way to do this is daily journaling. Sitting down for 5-30 minutes and evaluating your day or week and remembering the good, the bad, and the ugly by writing it down may serve as a sort of After Action Report (AAR) on your life at critical junctures. Figure out a simple and meaningful way to journal. I've often gone back into my journals and reviewed my notes to find insightful things I've forgotten or gotten out of focus.

When the work is done, improve the next cycle of clutter. I find the end result of my work is always rewarding, especially if I take the time to keep the important stuff in sight and relevant by discarding the junk effectively. I love how my desk looks and my custodian loves it too because he can wipe the whole surface again and see that the top is wood, not paper. The next realization is that I can impact the volume of the next "spring cleaning" task by setting up better processes for filing away clutter in "real-time" and keeping an uncluttered environment from which to work more consistently. I'm not suggesting I will ever have a consistently clear desk. I pride myself on being a "hands on" guy who moves about to be active with my students and teachers to ensure safety and engagement in the daily lives of my organization. I can; however, put into practice better disciplines to file away agendas more quickly and take daily or weekly moments to ensure the stacks don't build up and create the volume I've just experienced in the last cleaning cycle. In life, we should always live in balance. We need to balance the courage to push ourselves to be better and less cluttered with consideration of the fact that "life happens" and clutter is not always avoidable. What is avoidable; however, is allowing the clutter to impact the environment so much that you can't function efficiently amidst it.

Take some time for "spring cleaning." Do right by yourself by doing right with what you find. As you improve your processes and procedures with integrity, just remember the stack has to be tended a little at a time, as with the articulations of life's adjustments. Here a little, there a little, line upon line, precept upon precept. One step at a time. Give yourself the kick in the pants to do the work and the grace to break it down into manageable chunks. Clean well and live well. Perhaps they assist one another, the cleaning and the living.

LESSONS FROM THE FARM: LIFE IS LIKE GROWING TOBACCO

I have decided to write a brief parable about one of the stickiest topics I know. This writing is titled, "Lessons from the Farm: Life is Like Growing Tobacco." I know it may seem ironic to some that I would write an article about growing up farming this evil plant called tobacco. I learned a great deal about life in the tobacco fields of Colquitt County under the leadership and supervision of the three greatest male influencers: Donald Wayne (my dad), Ronald Wayman (my uncle and Dad's twin), and My Papa (also named Paul.) The tobacco fields were where I spent a large portion of my summers, especially after I was old enough to be useful in all phases of growing tobacco. My Papa and Uncle were the owners of the business in which their vocation was farming. One of their major cash crops during my formative years was tobacco. My focus will not be on these men or my relationships with them because such communication would bog me down for countless hours. I will say just mentioning them brings tears of joy and appreciation for all that Donald, Ronald, and Paul have instilled in me in the tobacco fields and barns. If there are any inaccuracies in my communication, I express my apologies now. My goal is not to teach anyone about the tobacco industry or how to farm; rather, to communicate some principles I learned on the farm that I believe to be relevant in living a *great* life.

Tobacco farming is a sticky job. I first entered tobacco fields with the job of pulling weeds around the young plants that were springing out of the ground in the hot fields of South Georgia. Temperatures were high throughout the days and nights, but the more work you could get done during the early and late hours, the better off you were. Dad took Shannon, my older sister (another great influencer in my life) and me to the fields in the evenings after work and in the mornings of weekends or days when he took off from his "day job." Dad was not a farmer by trade. He was the brother and son of the owners of the operation and he saw value in working and teaching us how to also work the farm. He would come home, take off his shirt and tie in exchange for field appropriate work clothes. We would be assigned a certain number of rows to examine for weeds and pull so the plants could grow and receive all nutrients and moisture from their environment without having to share it with invaders such as nut grass. This job could be boring and hot, but it could also be insightful as dad and I would often be able to talk about things because pulling weeds did not require a bridled concentration. Early in the growth of a plant you wish to harvest, you must take notice of invaders who threaten the attainment of the goal (harvest.) Dad had to make decisions on how many rows Shannon and I could effectively examine as well as making sure we could correctly identify weeds without disrupting the plant that was at home in those beds.

In the rows of your life, grow the many fruits you will bear during your time planted on earth. You will have many opportunities to make decisions about what is important to you. It is critical that you protect the early stages of growth from "invaders" like nut grass that would run rampant in the fields. You have to work to avoid the choking out of the crop. The nut grass we pulled is an interesting analogy in itself. On the surface, it is easy to break off and pull the nut grass invested in a weak tobacco leaf; however, the root is still anchored below for new growth to occur within a couple of weeks. It was critical we took time enough to be certain we got to the root of the plant so its removal was permanent. The nut grass was relentless in its pursuit of life. We were tasked with ending it. The two ways we accomplished this were via plow with carefully applied herbicide or hand removal (my most difficult application.) Either way, the main concern was to make sure you ended the life of one plant to preserve the life of the other.

How is life like pulling weeds in tobacco? You must know what the plant you wish to grow looks like when it emerges so you can identify and remove any invaders that threaten its life. Also be sure the applications and methods you use for such removal are beneficial rather than harmful to the plant. For example, if you try to kill nut grass by applying herbicides directly on top of tobacco, you could damage the crop. Apply carefully anytime you seek to utilize life's herbicides. The most common mistake I made on the farm was with larger weeds like the cocklebur. Because these invaders grew close to the tobacco plant and were large in size, I would uproot the crop with the weed. I recall doing this on more than one occasion. Quickly, frantically, and sometimes with great fear of getting caught, I would replant the mistakenly removed tobacco in its original hole by repacking the dirt around it making sure the tobacco plant was upright. Oftentimes I even said a little prayer in hopes of making sure the fruits of my labor had God's grace applied as well. I realized through observation that Dad, Uncle Ronald, and Papa occasionally had to employ the same strategy. This analogy is synonymous with one of Jesus' parables. I won't belabor the point because Jesus himself stressed not to ruin the harvest in our quest to destroy the invaders. We want to destroy invaders that threaten our harvest, but we must employ skillful wisdom to preserve the ultimate goal of a good harvest. Don't pull the good and bad by wantonly working when pulling weeds. In our life, the only source of skillful wisdom is in the Word of God. Utilize this resource to identify the invaders and the best methods for their removal. Utilize pastors, teachers, apostles, and prophets in your life to assist as well. In Colquitt County, we were blessed to have the University of Georgia trained (Go DAWGS!) extension agent who could help provide, without direct cost to the farmer, his expertise in many areas of protecting the harvest. The point is to carefully get out the weeds so they do not choke the tobacco or Word of God in your life.

The second major lesson I learned was the uniqueness of growing tobacco from a seed compared to other crops. See, tobacco is a transplanted crop. It is grown in one environment during a volatile season to be sold and planted in a different environment during the appropriate growing season. In the days I was involved, this meant fighting the elements of winter and providing a protective environment under plastic for the tobacco seeds to spring and break soil. We then harvested these plants and sold them to farmers to be subsequently planted in the fields they prepared. I remember times when we would have to go to these fields to replace the plastic to protect the plants from the harsh reality of freezing rains and winds. The plants had no protection. We had to provide it. The "claws" or plastic that protected these plants had to be maintained during a certain period which was hard work. This work was made more difficult because of the cold and windy conditions. Thank God for wisdom and the advent of the greenhouse. I wish the greenhouse had come more quickly. At least I was in school a lot of this time so I only experienced some of the frustrations that Papa and Uncle Ronald dealt with on a consistent basis. I will not spend a bunch of time describing the threats posed to this process of growing the plants from a seedling, but I will say there is a reason we are encouraged to add potting soil, additional nutrients, and high amounts of water during planting. I am convinced that the raising of children is a great comparison in this instance. When a child is in his/her formative years, it is critical they obtain the characteristic of self-discipline, submission to authority, understanding of important guiding principles, and the ability to pee and poop on the potty...I digress. Anyway, we must realize the process from seed to harvest has some critical stages and none are really more important than others, but the sensitivity and susceptible nature of the life we are concerned about can be important to recognize. Work diligently as a parent to "train up a child in the way he should go" and to recognize that "foolishness is bound up in the heart of a child" but the "rod of correction" will drive the foolishness "far from him," (Proverbs 22:15 KJV.) Don't lose sight of the end goal of the harvest and overcorrect and micromanage the life of the plant/child. Recognize the importance of the protection and impartations of nutrients that are critical in the early stages of growth whether you are talking about a child, the birth of an idea, or a project you are called to complete.

At the center of tobacco growth, I found the most hated task, "suckering." There were really two tasks that went hand and hand. These were topping and suckering. A farmer must "top," or snap off the flowering head, of the mature plant when it reaches between 4.5 to 6 feet in height. The desired breaking point is below the wimpy leaves but above the more mature looking ones. Topping assists with the stunting of growth, presumably so you don't have to hire Michael Jordan and other tall individuals to crop it (another term for harvesting the plant's leaves.) During and subsequent to this process there is another task that is needed called "suckering." I must say that "suckering" tobacco sucks. Oops, we don't say "sucks." Let's just say, "suckering tobacco stinks." It is a filthy job because suckers are the stickiest and newest growth in the tobacco plant that attempts to suck the life-giving nutrients in order to sustain their growth. Suckers almost act as new plants growing from the original stalk and the goal is to harvest high quality leaves that are already on the plant. Maintaining these leaves are the priority; therefore, removing the sucker also becomes a priority. This task is accomplished by walking down the rows of tobacco, identifying the sucker, and carefully pinching it out without damaging the leaf above it. This process is tedious work in the hot sun with sticky residue as its annoyant (made up this word on purpose, just go with it.) I hated the sticky feeling and learned we could put dirt on our hands to help, but then you just added a dirty feeling to the sticky feeling. Now you have a sweaty brow with sticky fingers that are caked with dirt. It was not fun.

This sub-parable is certainly the most powerful analogy in my opinion. Removing suckers is critical and their appearance in the final sheets of cooked tobacco added insult to injury as your price per pound was decreased. Suckers had to be removed because they stole vital nutrients and threatened the quality of the harvested leaves if they were cooked with the tobacco. Suckers are much greener and full of moisture and gook; therefore, if they are harvested with the tobacco, the value of the overall cured product is greatly reduced. No suckers allowed! There were many developments in the eradication of suckers in the plant. One such development had a few processes. First, you topped the plants. Second, you applied a poison that was strong enough to kill the sucker without destroying the stalk and its leaves. This product had to be applied by hand to be certain that the suckers received the lethal dose. Sprayers were fitted with boom arms and a hand nozzle so people could walk directly over each plant to apply herbicides. The operators had to time their spray so the liquid mixture would utilize gravity to flow to the bottom of the stalk assuring the farmer that all sucker growth areas would be impacted. This was very labor intensive and the poison was not cheap either, but it eliminated the multiple trips to the field to remove suckers throughout the growing season. I was thankful for such an innovation. I don't know how cost effective it was, but I enjoyed the minimized number of sticky, suckering trips back to these fields.

How does all this babble relate to life? Well, you may have already identified in your thoughts some suckers in your life. We have outgrowths critical to the success of our mission or purpose. These "leaves" are the end product we wish to be fruits of our life, but there are often unintended growths resulting from the propagation of the original plant. I don't know what yours may be, but I find my desire for perfection also produces many suckers like intense levels of frustration as my desire to reach perfection takes hits. I find my enjoyment of talking and preaching can be a great benefit, but I must learn to listen more earnestly without trying to preach or fix a problem (another sucker in my plant) if I want effectiveness in my most important relationships. I could go on forever identifying suckers in my life. Much like the admonishment of Jesus, I would like to encourage you to be careful to identify the suckers in your own life and not get overextended to identify the suckers in the lives of others. Sufficient to the day is the trouble thereof. Constantly revisit the methods and strategies you employ to remove the suckers. Work to improve the fruitfulness of the mission. The most important thing is not the removal of the sucker, but the assurance there is life in the leaf that is the harvest you desire. If you tear out the sucker wounding the leaf in the process, the mission is failed. Don't be suckered. Remove the suckers that keep you from your divine call. Life is about funneling all the resources into the correct pathway so this life is lived the right way. The proof is in the reaping of the harvest.

Once the tobacco plant reaches maturity and the suckers are

removed, we're ready to begin harvesting the bottom crop. The "sand lugs" are the leaves at the bottom of the plant that often remain dirty because of their location. Their location near the sand and the action of rain can cause these leaves to add to their bodies the charm of dirt. This dirt does devalue the end product, but a farmer must decide if he is going to harvest the leaves, knock them off and leave them in the field to be plowed, or leave them on the stalk to continue to rob nourishment from the stalk. I experienced carrying out the orders of cropping/harvesting and knocking them off. Oftentimes we would knock them off while harvesting the cleaner leaves above them. The market determined which strategy was best. I remember hating to crop the "sand lugs" because you spent back breaking time bending over and the sand would hit us in the face and get in our eyes while hanging it in the barns. Our lives often produce these "sand lugs." The great thing is that we can still receive benefits from the harvest of these subpar leaves. Just because there are tasks in life that seem dirtier and less fruitful, that does not mean the work to remove these lugs is not valuable. We must prioritize our lives in ways that often remove good things we do. Exercise is great and should be a part of our lives, but this activity can become a sand lug keeping us away from providing nutrients to other areas we may need to expend more energy and attention. See, I am now a husband, father, principal, teacher, and coach, but my workouts serve only as a contribution toward the goals accomplished in the other descriptors/areas of life. I am not a professional athlete or a fitness trainer. I must make sure the time and energy devoted to working out is commensurate with the outcomes I desire. If I was attempting to accomplish a victory in a forced MMA fight, it may be appropriate for me to expend more energy in the area of working out so I can continue to be a father and husband as a result of my avoidance of death or brain damage in the arena. However, wisdom would be to avoid the MMA fight and stick to contributing to growth in areas I'm called. Avoid the sand lugs. The best way to do this is to be sure you constantly evaluate your effectiveness in the areas of life you prioritize. Don't waste too much time doing good things that don't contribute to your greatness. Remove the lugs and get to the good parts of the stalk.

In the life of the tobacco plant, my favorite part of the job, when in the field, was "stripping." When you have harvested the lugs and some of the good leaves on the bottom, there comes a time when you can harvest all that is left. This is called "stripping." This does not involve getting naked. It involves collecting the rest of the leaves. Stripping is the fastest and brainless portion of the harvest. You just run your hands down the stalk, removing the remaining leaves and taking them to the racks for collection into the barn. This process provides great satisfaction because it is quick and doesn't take as long to fill a barn during this phase. I liken this part of the tobacco growing season to the season in life when you seem to be working most frantically with the end in sight. There are times in our daily walk when we can honestly say we are making progress. Stripping means you are getting close to the end of the season. In the life of a teacher, this is usually March and April. You are getting students ready to ace their End of Course Assessment. For an accountant, I would assume this would be the same time as for a teacher because of the April 15th filing deadline.

In the field, a skillful hand would figure out the quickest way to get the most leaves and gather them under his/her non-cropping arm. As a right-hander, I would strip the stalk with my right hand and move that hand quickly to gather the leaves by slapping the open hand underneath the open left arm where I would clamp down on these leaves and any previously placed there. As I reached my left arm capacity, I would kick up my left knee to help pack in more tobacco so my number of trips to the trailer could be reduced. Then, when capacity was truly reached, I would get one last grasp with my right arm and bear hug the total as I delivered it to the trailer. We all took pride in the size of the load and the speed with which we could deliver it to the trailer. In life, healthy competition is not about beating someone or some entity, but rather about doing your best and utilizing teamwork and competition to make yourself better. I often enjoyed Papa's or Uncle Ronald's evaluation of my work because I did push myself to work hard and do what I could to take pride in the tasks I accomplished. I hated to ask too many questions or to have to ask for help because I was unable to finish the job. It is with great pride and contentment that I can say that I was as good of a worker for Papa and Uncle Ronald as anyone else on that farm. I cared about working fast, working hard, working right, and finishing the job.

I was taught to be the best I could be. I remember being fairly good at all the jobs done by the time I was sixteen years old. John and I were a great team and we always helped do every job so our goal of harvesting a barn was reached as quickly as possible. In life we should always strive to learn how to work hard in the most efficient ways to reach our goals. Our goals should be the same as the people for whom we work. I wanted to make Papa and Uncle Ronald proud. I remember driving the tractor was my first job under the supervision of Papa. This job involved pulling the trailer up at a pace consistent with the speed of the 6-8 croppers who were harvesting the tobacco. I was to pay careful attention to the workers cropping the tobacco so I could keep the trailer near without running over them in the process. I recall one comical moment that was most importantly characterized with great fear in the outset. Leon was definitely an alcoholic with a somewhat inconsistent disposition. I recall, on the day of this story, his disposition was one of irritability married with a great humor. In other words, he was drunk. I did not know this at the time. He was placing tobacco on the trailer right in front of a tire. When I had turned around to make sure all was clear, he was not in sight (I swear he was not); however, when I pulled forward, I was commanded to stop and watch what I was doing. I immediately braked and depressed the clutch to stop the tractor. When I had disengaged the gear, I turned around to hear some adjectives, not used by any of my family members, combined with some I knew to be avoided when self-control was not in question. Leon was cussing me out because I had run over his foot. I was horrified because I genuinely cared about the people I worked with on the farm. My horror turned into a combination of fear and terror as Leon reached into his pack pocket. I had been viewing the top end of this pocket insert throughout the morning with the deduction that such an ornate knob could only be the top of a nice, big knife. This was the knife that Leon would utilize to seek retribution for this foolish thirteen-year old's inattentive mistake. I was getting ready to dismount the tractor and utilize my exceptional speed to run when I was enlightened the use of ornate dressings attract alcoholics to the bottle. Leon was opening up his ornate flask to relieve his pain through a snort on his bottle of whiskey. I still don't know the type or the brand, but I was relieved that I would grow to be a man. I learned things are not always as they appear and just when you think your mistakes are producing fruits you cannot handle or bear, you will find there is a way of escape. It's never as bad as you think when emotions are in control.

I was often embarrassed by mistakes made while learning to do the tasks associated with growing and harvesting tobacco. One time, while driving the Ford F350, I was delivering the final trailer to the barns. We should have all been excited about the imminent completion of the barn as the ladies, teaming with John and me, were fast at unloading the trailers. One problem remained. I ran the front right tire of the truck into a sharp corner of the racking table because of my desire to get the trailer closer. This caused a puncture in the tire as well as aggravation, expense, and delay. Everyone tried to make me feel alright, but I remember the disappointment in myself for the inattentiveness and lack of diligence. Diligence does not just include working hard. It is working hard while paying attention to what matters so you get the job done right. Papa and Dad both used to say, "If it's worth doing, it's worth doing right." See, I learned a lot while growing tobacco.

I also learned how to communicate with hard-headed people who spoke a different language than me. Stephen Covey says, "Seek first to understand, then to be understood." I was not in this mode one particular day at the farm. We were trying out a new crew of workers who spoke Spanish. My assumption is they were from Mexico, but I did not view their identification, so I can't confirm such an assumption. The hot-headed gentleman working with me hanging tobacco (putting the racks full of tobacco in the barn) spoke no English. I had mostly mastered the language myself, but had not mastered the art of sign language apparently. I tried to help him understand how to hang the tobacco without creating problems, but he kept doing the same things causing the racks of tobacco to fall on me. I attempted to get a translator to clear up our miscommunication, but that was to no avail. I don't know if he really wanted to fix the problem. I was vested, but he was not. The same incident occurred one time too many to a normally very peaceful teenager. I was determined, after another incident (the final straw), to clearly communicate my message. After being cut on the top of my chest as a result of his unwillingness to follow directions in English and Spanish, I chose to communicate in physical sign language. I took the slat that had busted open on the rack of tobacco and used it to pin him against the wall of the barn. I spoke with clarity in a language (though uninterpretable) that seemed to bring understanding. It was becoming clear to him I was unhappy with his continuous lack of patience in following my lead. I may not be as old as him, but I was willing to ensure that I would gain his respect. Upon picking up the busted rack from the barn floor and loading it on the rack myself, I was met with the swing of an iron slat used to keep the tobacco in the racks. His assault... and the results...are not pertinent to my point. Suffice it to say I was taught by my dad not to fight unless "what was being fought for was worth dying for." The rest of the story is classified and not something I am sure should be interpreted as a good or bad outcome. I did learn that sometimes you have to communicate in ways you wish you did not, but the truth is that only metal can penetrate the sense into some hard heads. The value in this story is really small, but it is a story I will never forget.

I learned so much on the farm while growing tobacco. In closing, I would like to say that the harvest was exciting. The best time of year was when we'd stripped the last field and filled the last barns. We would celebrate with a special lunch prepared by Grandma and Papa. Papa cooked the meat and Grandma and Aunt Elaine prepared the sides. I loved some dead cow. We would sometimes have fried fish and sometimes steak. This celebration was something to look forward to after every season. I think it was interesting how some workers would get disgruntled over pay and may not benefit from the end of the year celebration because they would quit, but Papa just fed those who were there at the end. Make sure you finish what you start so you can enjoy the fruits of labor whether its products were intended to benefit you or your boss.

If you are reading this, it is highly probable you are aware that I am not Jesus and thus lack the ability to tell a parable to the level of accuracy and application He can. Forgive me for any incomplete analogies and thoughts. I hope this writing is, at least, intriguing.

Perhaps it will engage you in a way that causes you to think about lessons learned in your life. A weakness, perhaps gained in the low precision training of growing tobacco, is the fact I like to finish what I start. As a result, much like a day in the tobacco fields, the racks of tobacco needed to be balanced and not packed too tightly or too loosely. Too tight meant that the tobacco wouldn't cook and cure evenly while too loose meant you would waste a great deal of space and energy in the barn and in human resources because people were paid for the labor to fill a barn. I chose not to continue packing it in as I must do some other things, but I wanted to close the door on this barn for now. I may choose, at some point, to come back and edit. Grant me the grace, if I do not, to enjoy the read and learn what you can from my experiences of growing up and growing tobacco on the farm. I have reaped a great life harvest from the experiences in those formative years. Thank you to Mom, Dad, Papa, Uncle Ronald, and all of my family with whom I was able to share so many special moments in this parable/analogy.

V

DAILY DEVOTIONALS

BE STRONG AND COURAGEOUS

> "Courage is not simply one of the virtues, but the form
> of every virtue at the testing point."
>
> — C.S. LEWIS

One of my favorite passages in the Bible is Joshua 1:5-9. Here, Joshua is getting ready to begin leading after Moses' death, and God's message to Joshua has 2 major parts: Encouragement and Direction.

Read this passage and let's delve in.

> *"There shall not any man be able to stand before thee all the days*
> *of thy life: as I was with Moses, so I will be with thee: I will*
> *not fail thee, nor forsake thee. Be strong and of a good*
> *courage: for unto this people shalt thou divide for an*
> *inheritance the land, which I sware unto their fathers to*
> *give them. Only be thou strong and very courageous, that*
> *thou mayest observe to do according to all the law, which*
> *Moses my servant commanded thee: turn not from it to the*
> *right hand or to the left, that thou mayest prosper*
> *whithersoever thou goest. This book of the law shall not*

*depart out of thy mouth; but thou shalt meditate therein day
and night, that thou mayest observe to do according to all
that is written therein: for then thou shalt make thy way
prosperous, and then thou shalt have good success. Have not I
commanded thee? Be strong and of a good courage; be not
afraid, neither be thou dismayed: for the Lord thy God is
with thee whithersoever thou goest."*

— JOSHUA 1:5-9 KJV

"Be strong and of good courage...be thou strong and very
courageous...Be strong and of a good courage..."

Three specific times, Joshua is encouraged, and given directions as
well.

1. Be strong and of good courage - God has not changed His
   mind about the land He swore to give to them; it's time for
   Joshua to lead the people in as one of the faithful spies who
   returned with a good report of God's promised land.
   Consider God's promises and encourage yourself with them.
2. Only be thou strong and very courageous - Strength and
   courage are key ingredients to effective Kingdom living; we
   are summoned to observe and obey according to God's
   commands. Jesus simplified Moses' commands for us (love
   the Lord your God with all your heart, soul, mind and
   strength and your neighbor as yourself.) This summoning of
   courage continues with the directions to meditate on God's
   Word so you are able to do according to all that is written
   (Jesus overcame that way..."it is written.") Observing to do or
   obedience to God's Word comes with a promised result of
   prosperity and good success.
3. Have I not commanded thee? Be strong and of good
   courage; be not afraid, neither be thou dismayed - This is a
   reminder God is with us wherever we go. When the Word is
   in our heart through meditation and studying to do what is
   written, we are positioned for "taking the land promised."

We obey the Word we take with us...God is with us wherever we go and He will go before us and prepare the way in...out...around...through! Be strong and courageous...God wants to lead you to your promised land. Be strong and courageous...God has ways better than ours that will lead to prosperity and success. Be strong and courageous...God is with you, wherever you go! Be strong and courageous as you grow in the knowledge of God and His will for your life. Do things His way and correct your course anytime you recognize you've missed steps. God is with you! You matter...Do what matters...

Prayer

Heavenly Father, I thank you for your love and who you have chosen to be in my life. You promised to never leave or forsake me. Help me to demonstrate courage in my life. You have not given me a spirit of fear, but of power, love, and a sound mind. Help me to be strong and courageous as I take dominion over all that you have given me to influence. As I commit to study to do according to your word, make my way prosperous and give me success. Your kingdom and your will be done in my life in ways that cause heaven to influence earth. I believe the One I pray to is able to do exceedingly abundantly beyond what I could ask or think. I believe, help THOU my unbelief! Amen.

FULL COMMITMENT

"Practice self-awareness, self-evaluation, and self-improvement. If we are aware that our manners - language, behavior, and actions - are measured against our values and principles, we are able to more easily embody the philosophy, leadership is a matter of how to be, not how to do."

— FRANCES HESSELBEIN

"Jesus said unto him, Thou shalt love the Lord thy God with all thy heart, and with all thy soul, and with all thy mind. This is the first and great commandment. And the second is like unto it, Thou shalt love thy neighbour as thyself. On these two commandments hang all the law and the prophets."

— MATTHEW 22:37-40 KJV

This reality is such a simple truth yet it reaches every part of purpose and vision of who we should be as a people and how we should live. We are wonderfully created beings who are endowed by our Creator with the gifts articulated by Frances Hesselbein which are self-awareness, self-evaluation, and self-improvement. A commitment to work on each and develop in us the stamina to continuously improve will assist in making us fit to lead. We identify desires, gifts, and purpose within us and how they relate to what is going on around us in life. We are able to evaluate what we know and expand the reaches of that knowledge, understanding, and wisdom so we continuously grow. We take what we are aware of and make adjustments in our life that help improve our position in reality. We commit to adjust our "language, behavior, and actions" so we reflect the purposes of the One who made us. We are capable of recognizing deep growth within our soul, not just from actions. Regardless of who we are and how deep in a hole we become, we can recognize principles because they are timeless and self-evident. Jesus' communication is the linchpin of all the "law and prophets" or rules by which we should live. We are to love God with our heart, soul, and mind (the body will automatically follow) and we are to love our neighbor as ourselves. We must grasp the principle that there is One God and He is to be loved with all of our being. This love should influence how we treat others. We should love God and recognize that He is God. John tells us we demonstrate our love for Him by doing what He says.

Jesus' second command says that these two fulfill all of the law and to "love your neighbor as yourself." The key often overlooked in this statement is that you must love yourself. You must have enough awareness to recognize the loveliness of you as a creation of Him. You must respect yourself and who God has made you to be in order to be able to lead yourself to help and serve others.

Take time to think deeply about these two principles of love that are the essence of all human life.

1. God is supreme and created all things. Recognize Him for who He is and seek to obey.
2. Life of service begins with a realization that our faith works by love and we must demonstrate that love throughout His creation.

We are the starting point; however, we are not the end point. We impact the lives of those we are called to influence because of His life in us. We must seek first the Kingdom of God and align our lives in such a way that we are good ambassadors of that Kingdom. We should influence others with the same love He demonstrated by giving His only son. Love God, Love Self, and Love Others. Do it all how He said . Take time to reflect on who He is, who you are, and who you can serve. God bless you as you develop the commitment to live in obedience to the core commandment and to be a doer of what you believe. You matter...do what matters...

Prayer

Heavenly Father, I come to you appreciating your creative work in my life. I am fearfully and wonderfully made by your hands and am your workmanship created in Christ Jesus unto GOOD WORKS! Help me to demonstrate consistency in representing you by being obedient to your commands and serving others well. I love you with all my heart, soul, mind and strength. Again, I say, I love you with all of my heart, all of my soul, all of my mind, and all of my strength. I appreciate who you have made me to be and I ask you to help me love my neighbor as myself.

Come Holy Spirit, have your way in my life and do what is pleasing in your sight! Amen.

OVERCOMING

 "There is a time in the life of every problem when it is
big enough to see, yet small enough to solve."

— MIKE LEAVITT

*"Nay, in all these things we are made more than conquerors
through him that loved us."*

— ROMANS 8:37 KJV

We all face problems that sometimes look bigger than they really are. I often get accused of "making mountains out of molehills." Challenges, testing, trials of all kinds hit us on a regular basis. We often face problems that we can't even see. Regardless of the challenges, it is great to know that we have Romans 8:37 in our heart and as a promise that His love for us is present. I've often attempted challenges that were bigger than I felt prepared. In the fall of 2018, I took on the challenge of running my first ultra marathon. The event was the Duncan Ridge Trail 50K. This race is part of the Appalachian Trail and boasts 10,500 feet of elevation gain in the approximately 32 miles of travel (per my Garmin.) My first attempt of this event was four weeks removed from a high grade tear on my left thigh's adductor muscle. And because of a kickball game injury, I was unable to train for four weeks only giving me seven days before the 50K to practice my long distance running. I remember a moment when I was tempted to quit and my friends, Blake and Chadd Wright, were encouraging me as much as they could to just keep moving. I wound up telling them to run on ahead so they would not get caught at the midpoint's cutoff time. I used this time alone to refocus and break the rest of my race down into manageable parts. I ran to the next tree, leaned on the tree, got some water, and kept going. One time, I leaned on a tree that was not there and fell to the ground. That felt pretty good, lying on the ground. I didn't complete the race that year because I was five or six minutes beyond the cutoff at the half-way point of the race. I still ran 17 miles in extremely elevated terrain with an injury that probably should have sidelined me. I did go back and complete the race the next year with a better mindset and fitter body. I learned in this race to be an overcomer and break the race down into the most basic parts. Sometimes we look too far ahead and see that the top of the mountain looks like it is really a long way. The journey of 1,000 miles starts with the first step and the feeling during those early steps often overwhelms us. When life throws challenges that are steep and you feel like the problem is one of those that is not small enough to solve, break things down into the simplest parts and "just keep swimming." Don't forget you are more than a conqueror because the greater one lives inside of you and all you need to do to overcome is keep moving in the right direction. In the words of Chadd Wright, "Take quitting off the table." You are a conqueror. You matter...do what matters!

Prayer

Heavenly Father, I am so grateful to be more than a conqueror through Christ Jesus my Lord! I come before you humbly to request that you help me see what is before me clearly enough to walk in steps that are ordered by you, Lord. Your word is a lamp unto my feet and light unto my path. I thank you that my steps are ordered by You and I will not fail. I submit my will and my ways to Yours and ask that you lead, guide and direct me so that I am able to seek first Your Kingdom and have confidence that you will add what I need unto me! Thank you, God that you are more than enough and you do exceedingly abundantly above all I could ask or think! Amen.

PLAY BY THE RULES ON PURPOSE

"There are three constants in life...change, choice, and principles."

— STEPHEN COVEY

"I beseech you therefore, brethren, by the mercies of God, that ye present your bodies a living sacrifice, holy, acceptable unto God, which is your reasonable service. And be not conformed to this world: but be ye transformed by the renewing of your mind, that ye may prove what is that good, and acceptable, and perfect, will of God."

— ROMANS 12:1-2 KJV

"Keep the rules and keep your life; careless living kills. We humans keep brainstorming options and plans, but God's purpose prevails,"

— PROVERBS 19:16, 21 MSG

I f this statement by Dr. Covey is true, how we live with these "constants" is important. May we intentionally ensure our change always brings growth and transformation and not weak capitulation. Consider Romans 12:2. We are to be transformed by the renewing of our mind and not conformed to the world around us. If choice is a constant, we must take advantage of this power of choice and ensure our choices align with the constant of positive change and principles. Our choices are seeds planted to produce results. What will ours lead to? The constant of principles is one worthy of great attention. Principles, unlike change, are very predictable once we discover the truth. Align your choices and change with constant principles so your life will be anchored to something solid. Gravity is a principle that is truth, and knowledge of its impact teaches us much about our environment. May we experience a day full of positive growth and change where our life's choices are rooted in principles that govern effectiveness. Live by God's rules and your life will avoid the pitfalls of the careless. God is not moved by our choices and plans except when they align with His immutable laws and truth. My pastor, James Cordell, often says that "choices lead, feelings follow." I like to say our emotions make great servants but terrible leaders. Don't let your emotions and flaky feelings direct you, especially in times of challenge. Identify the key principles and make choices consistent with those. Your choices matter...you matter...do what matters!

Prayer

Heavenly Father, I thank you that you gave me the choice to choose who I will serve. I choose You. Help me to be the living sacrifice I am supposed to be and help me to renew my mind by your word so that I am transformed by your Word instead of conforming to the world around me. The word of God is spirit and life. Come Holy Spirit and have your purposes and plans manifested in every area of my life and my family's life. Amen.

CRY BABIES

"When you were born, you cried and the whole world rejoiced. Live life so that when you die, the whole world cries and you rejoice."

— NATIVE AMERICAN PROVERB: CHEROKEE

"And, having made peace through the blood of his cross, by him to reconcile all things unto himself; by him, I say, whether they be things in earth, or things in heaven. And you, that were sometime alienated and enemies in your mind by wicked works, yet now hath he reconciled In the body of his flesh through death, to present you holy and unblameable and unreproveable in his sight: To whom God would make known what is the riches of the glory of this mystery among the Gentiles; which is Christ in you, the hope of glory."

— COLOSSIANS 1:20-22, 27 KJV

This proverb is simple and to the point, but what a way to think about life. Live it in a way that, when you die, the whole world cries and you rejoice. We rejoice because of the truth that, when we die, we have this hope of a greater life of eternal glory in heaven as a result of the blood of the cross. Jesus came to make sure you and I were reconciled, made right, and given access to His righteousness. We are not our own, but we are bought by this work of Jesus. This wonderful love that he has loved us with is the greatest. He, while we were still in rebellion, gave His life that we may have peace with the Father because of His work.

Through His obedience to crucify His flesh on our behalf, we have the treasure of His presence in our earthen vessel through the Holy Spirit's coming. Live in such a way that welcomes this companionship so you can have a testimony that praises Him, gives glory to God through the work He demonstrates through you, and causes you to be full of joy because of Whose presence you enter. When my father in-law passed away, the city allowed us to use the downtown theater because they were concerned about the traffic and problems with the funeral home being able to house the numbers attending and wanting to pay their respects. The community that represented his world certainly cried a great deal and we celebrated his life with a beautiful service preceded by visitation that was so crowded, many had to give up and be turned away in order for us to be able to start the service on time. His wife often says to me that "he left nothing unsaid and nothing undone. He was proud of his life and what he'd accomplished." Those words comfort me on a regular basis, but they also serve as a reminder to be intentional about how I live so my "dash" in life is worth crying for when I meet Jesus.

He paid a price, so you don't have to!

Believing is your access into this grace...

Confession brings the power to live his ways!

Balance this idea of grace or undeserved favor with the power of sowing the right seeds so you reap a harvest. Walk by faith, do the work, watch Him Work! You matter...do what matters!

Prayer

Heavenly Father, I come to you in prayer to ask you to help me live in ways that demonstrate worthy pursuits of excellence that are consistent with your heavenly influences and kingdom purposes. Help me to demonstrate that Christ in me is my only hope for any glory. Come Holy Spirit and influence my life so I am able to glorify His name in how I live. I am saved by grace through faith and I ask you, Lord, to help me walk in the kind of faithful obedience that pleases you. Come Holy Spirit and have your way in my life! Amen.

LET THIS MIND BE IN YOU

"True humility-the basis of the Christian system-is the low but deep and firm foundation of all virtues."

— EDMUND BURKE

"Don't look out only for your own interests, but take an interest in others, too. You must have the same attitude that Christ Jesus had. Though he was God, he did not think of equality with God as something to cling to. Instead, he gave up his divine privileges; he took the humble position of a slave and was born as a human being. When he appeared in human form, he humbled himself in obedience to God and died a criminal's death on a cross. Therefore, God elevated him to the place of highest honor and gave him the name above all other names, that at the name of Jesus every knee should bow, in heaven and on earth and under the earth, and every tongue declare that Jesus Christ is Lord, to the glory of God the Father."

— PHILIPPIANS 2:4-11 NLT

I t's so easy when life gets stressful to do the opposite of what Paul is teaching here. We are stressed and just want to "get mine." We forget, as leaders and as disciples, the number one discipline and influence technique is humility. Humility is a foundational virtue allowing us to bow low that we may lift up truth. Humility brings honor and glory. Christ humbled himself. He took on so what will you take on today? Will you take on the world? Will you take on this great challenge? Will you take on the FORM OF A SERVANT? Let this mind...let this mind...let this mind be in you...What mind? The mind of a humble servant who washed His disciples feet, who took on the beatings, bruises, battering, shame of being spat upon, made fun of, laid bare in an agonizing death in front of others, dragging a cross through the streets like a criminal. He was wounded for our transgressions and He was bruised for our iniquity. The chastisement of our peace was upon Him and by His Stripes, we WERE healed. We are instructed to let the mind that was obedient to that pain and suffering be in us. There is great reward in following Christ. I believe God wants us blessed and He wants the fruit of our labors to be good and wholesome; however, we can't expect to live for ourselves and forget we are to humbly serve. Discipline self to humble self. No greater love hath any man than this, he lay down his life for his FRIENDS. Jesus called us friends. We must honor that friendship and be his companion by taking on the same mindset. He was a humble servant, but don't forget that He boldly spoke the truth, kicked the devil in the mouth, healed the sick, and delivered people from a fruitless life. Go humbly yet boldly into the world and preach the gospel and, when necessary, use words! Let this mind be in you...You matter...do what matters...

Prayer

Heavenly Father, I come to you humbly and recognize my inability to do much of what matters without your help. I boldly confess that I can do all things through Christ who strengthens me. I know that I, in my own self, can do nothing of worth. I humble myself under Your mighty hand and wait faithfully for You to exalt me and give me honor as you see fit. Help me to obey and demonstrate my love for You through consistent obedience. I ask that You build my reputation and resume so I prosper in doing your kingdom work. Come Holy Spirit, have your way in my life and do what you want to in my life and with my life. Amen.

THE POWER OF THE SPOKEN WORD

> "The thought that's in your mind is not real and has no power until you speak it."

— CHADD WRIGHT - U.S. NAVY SEAL, RETIRED

"Let no corrupt communication proceed out of your mouth, but that which is good to the use of edifying, that it may minister grace unto the hearers."

— EPHESIANS 4:29 KJV

"Death and life are in the power of the tongue: and they that love it shall eat the fruit thereof."

— PROVERBS 18:21 KJV

Chadd Wright often talks about how he was in BUDS and one of his buddies was just as fit and able, but that man started talking about the negative thoughts in his mind and he wound up quitting the next morning. Chadd uses this example to reinforce "the power of the spoken word." You can have bad thoughts attacking your mind, but they have no power until they are actually spoken into the world we live. One of the first scriptures I was taught as a young child was a scripture in Ephesians. Mom had me commit it to memory and I had to figure out the words corrupt, edifying, proceed, and minister. This scripture can stand alone as one of the most important reminders of the Christian walk. Don't let your powerful speech be hijacked by the enemy corrupting the important communication from your mouth. You are able to speak life and death because of the creative power of your tongue. Our words should be good, useful, and edifying so people are built up and encouraged by what we say. Our words are to accomplish the purpose of ministering or serving grace to those who hear them. Ask yourself, when I speak, are people built up and encouraged by my words? Are people ministered by my words even when they have not earned it? Do my words align with the word of God so the fruit of my lips is sure to produce the fruit of righteousness? The first step in controlling your tongue is recognizing the importance and appreciating the real potential of this opportunity you possess. "Death and life are in the power of the tongue" and you eat its fruit regularly. Why not take control of that source so life is the fruit, encouragement is the norm, and edifying is the result? You matter...your words matter...speak what matters...

Prayer

Heavenly Father, I know that death and life are in the power of the tongue and You want me to choose life. I ask for the help of You, Holy Spirit, to discipline my communication so it encourages, edifies and ministers grace to those who hear it. I ask that Your grace minister to me in such a way that the fruit of Your ministry is reflected in how I talk and how I live. Come Holy Spirit and have Your way in mouth and in my life. Make my speech align with your truth so I experience Your life all the days of my life! Amen.

CREATION SPEAKS

"I love to think of nature as an unlimited broadcasting station, through which God speaks to us every hour, if we will only tune in."

— GEORGE WASHINGTON CARVER

"For the invisible things of him from the creation of the world are clearly seen, being understood by the things that are made, even his eternal power and Godhead; so that they are without excuse: Because that, when they knew God, they glorified him not as God, neither were thankful; but became vain in their imaginations, and their foolish heart was darkened. Professing themselves to be wise, they became fools, And changed the glory of the incorruptible God into an image made like to corruptible man, and to birds, and four footed beasts, and creeping things."

— ROMANS 1:20-23 KJV

Mr. Carver was able to see different uses for a simple thing we call the peanut. With the combination of pea growing from the vine and nuts having a protective shell guarding the meat, peanuts serve many purposes and I would imagine its discovery and uses scope way beyond the peanut itself. He is most known for his farm bulletins with 105 food recipes using peanuts; however, he was much more than a researcher and professor. He reverenced the power of nature to provide food and resources to its inhabitants. He believed that "if you love it enough, anything will talk to you." Well, I wonder how much we recognize and listen as God speaks to us. Do we slow down enough to recognize the voice of God crying out in the beauty and vastness of His creation? Do we worship our abilities to create new ideas and new things more than we worship the creator who made all things? Do we become fools and trade in the glory (real and tangible weight of truth revealed) of an incorruptible God for an image made by his very own creation? How much do we know God and know about Him, yet ignore that knowledge or act in ways inconsistent with truth? May we calm ourselves and love Him enough to listen so we can hear Him talk. He talks through His Word. He talks through the consistency of everyday natural laws we see/observe in nature, and he talks in a still small voice. Are we still enough to hear? God be praised in our observation and communication. Be blessed and enjoy creation, but don't worship it. Worship Him! You matter...do things that matter...

Prayer

Heavenly Father, Your creation cries out praises to You continually. I give You praise with the fruit of my lips and I ask that You help me to always praise and worship rightly the things that are praiseworthy. Help me to never fail to see the beautiful lessons Your creation wants to teach me and to never praise the creation, but only the Creator. I confess that all things are held together by the Word of Your power and that all creation was made by You and for You and Your glory. May my life praise you in its everyday glory. You have made me fearfully and wonderfully. My lips will praise You, my choices will follow You, and my eyes will look to the heavens for the help that only you can provide. Amen.

A MERRY HEART

> "For human beings, simply put, the default state is
> happiness. If you don't believe me, spend a little time
> with a human fresh from the factory, an infant or toddler.
> Obviously, there's a lot of crying and fussing associated
> with the start-up phase of little humans, but the fact is,
> as long as their most basic needs are met—no immediate
> hunger, no immediate fear, no scary isolation, no physical
> pain or enduring sleeplessness—they live in the moment,
> perfectly happy."

— MO GAWDAT IN SOLVE FOR HAPPY

*"A merry heart does good, like medicine, but a broken spirit dries
the bones."*

— PROVERBS 17:22 NKJV

Our default state is happy, according to Mo Gawdat. I really
enjoyed reading his book *Solve for Happy: Engineering Your Path to
Discovering the Joy Inside of You*. The very title tells a great story of the
difference between happiness and joy. Happiness is based on

circumstances and my expectations regarding them, but joy is a fruit of the spirit. Joy is based on the truth of the character and nature of spiritual forces while happiness is based on interpretation from five physical senses. I love this scripture from Proverbs. It's been one that my wife and I have quoted for years with the kids to start off the "ABC scriptures." (Those are scriptures memorized for each letter of the alphabet.) This verse starts it all off and I think this scripture has the potential to start the revival in our hearts and lives if we choose joy. The Bible teaches us the Joy of the Lord is our strength and in His presence is fullness of joy. We are taught Jesus wants to take up residence in our heart through the third person of the trinity, the Holy Spirit. As we think in our heart, so are we. Dry bones are dead bones. We don't want to be there. A merry heart is the opposite of the place we find ourselves when we are led/guided by our emotions. If we are governed by how we feel about what we observe instead of being guided by the Hope of Christ, our outlook is less likely to be governed by a merry heart. A merry heart is not determined by circumstances, but by choice. There are many who face life's challenges with joy and positivity. There are also multitudes who whine about everything. Facebook is the home of negativity. The news gives plenty of fuel to the fire. David, in I Samuel 30 when Ziklag was burned and their women and children were taken, encouraged himself in the Lord until he got courage to go after what he desired and God redeemed what the enemy took at the hands of David's band of ruffians. God is able; therefore, you are able through Him to do His purposes as He will give you strength. What a place of peace from which to build a joyful heart. Keep your heart in the mode of joy and be merry. Expect God to work on your behalf in spite of challenges, tests, or circumstances. Those are just opportunities to get stronger, overcome, and mature. Remember, "A merry heart does good like a medicine, but a broken spirit dries up the bone." Don't be broken, take your medicine daily. Check out what the Word says about you and who you are, encourage yourself in the Lord, and re-joy your merry heart daily! You matter...do what matters...

Prayer

Heavenly Father, I know in Your presence is fullness of joy and this joy is my source of strength. Help me to guard my heart and mind with the truth of Your thoughts. I know Your thoughts are higher than mine and your ways are as well, but I receive the promise of the Spirit and His impact on me so I have the mind of Christ. Help me to think right, talk right, and live right as I rejoice in the Lord always! Amen.

THINK BEFORE YOU SPEAK

> My father had warned me, "Don't babble. Don't bray.
> For you never can tell who might hear what you say."
> My father had warned me, "Boy, button your lip."
> And I guess that I should have. I made a bad slip.

— -FROM "STEAK FOR SUPPER" DR. SEUSS

"Watch your words and hold your tongue; you'll save yourself a lot of grief."

— THE MESSAGE PROVERBS 21:23

"Whoever guards his mouth and tongue keeps his soul from troubles."

— PROVERBS 21:23 NKJV

This quote comes from a book of "Seuss-isms" that are simple yet appropriate. How often do we slow down and evaluate if our mouth is just running because it can? How often do we talk incessantly without really evaluating the quality of our speech? The Bible speaks of the power of our tongue, our words, and the importance we control our speech. James warns us to control our words like a bit in a horse's mouth or the rudder of a ship (James 3:3-4 KJV.) Jesus tells us in the Gospels that good fruit and bad fruit shouldn't come out of the same mouth and that life and death, blessing and curses are spoken. Proverbs tells us we eat the good of the land by the words of our mouth. We are justified and condemned by our words. Paul tells us we should "let no corrupt communication proceed out of our mouth (Ephesians 4:29 KJV)" but our words should edify and minister grace. Our mouth is a powerful vessel and we need help to make sure it doesn't "slip."

If we think before we speak, perhaps then our words will not be weak.

If our words are used with care, perhaps love will meet us there.

Our tongue no man can tame, but with God's help we can refrain...

From using words to wound and speaking what's untrue.

In His image we are made to speak what we want to see,

So let's tame our tongue with God's help so that we can be who we're to be!

Let this short poem remind you of the importance of thinking about your words. Think before you speak! Your words matter...say what matters...

Prayer

Heavenly Father, I am thankful for the power of my thoughts and my words. Help me to be responsible with both these tools you have created in me. I will watch my words to ensure they are carefully spoken to build up and create rather than to degrade and tear down. You said that You watch over Your words to perform them. Help me to invest in knowing your Words so I know how you perform so I can become more like You. May my thoughts and words be guarded in such a way that I don't allow the fruit of my lips to create trips and slips. I will speak in line with truth from the Word of God and the meditation of my heart. Amen.

CHOP YOUR OWN WOOD

"Chop your own wood, and it will warm you twice."

— HENRY FORD

"Stay calm; mind your own business; do your own job. You've heard all this from us before, but a reminder never hurts. We want you living in a way that will command the respect of outsiders, not lying around sponging off your friends."

— 1 THESSALONIANS 4:11-12 MSG

Henry Ford said, "Chop your own wood and it will warm you twice." This passage is more than that, but it is critical we take some initiative to mind our own business and do our own job. It takes enough energy to do your own work well enough without any distracting, misplaced focus. Some simple advice for living in this verse...a reminder that never hurts... Work hard to stay in motion and keep up the good work. Renew your mind daily to stay focused on the right work. Keep a worthy "end in mind." Stay calm so your work doesn't suffer from the invasions of displaced emotions. Your brain works most logically when you are not stressed. Your results may speed up under stress, but that stress induced work may suffer. Plan ahead and be purposeful in your chopping. Discipline yourself in your mind and in your mouth and your motions will follow. Spirit led, soul fed, body dead (alive in Christ, but dead to the carnal pleasures that distract.) As a leader, one of the most difficult tasks is the chore of sorting. We must sort the priorities and sort the responsibilities. We have to be able to delegate tasks based on abilities and passions and be diligent enough to hold on to the tasks we need to lead. Jocko Willink wrote about "extreme ownership" and the importance of the power of our leadership influence and responsibility (I recommend you read their book entitled *Extreme Ownership*.) The buck stops with you regarding the results of your life and your organization's progress under your influence. Don't try to do everything, but what you do...do well and do it diligently so its results will glorify your Boss...Creator...King! Chop away today and be warmed by your work. Your work matters...do the work that matters...

Prayer

Heavenly Father, praise to Your name and all that comes with Your presence in my life. Help me to chop away at the right things in my life so my work creates momentum toward more work that glorifies you. Help me to stay calm, meditate on your truth, and be at peace. Help me to seek first Your kingdom and righteousness so my work produces the things that glorify you. Lead me not into temptations that distract and cause strife. Deliver me from evil. I will work to diligently seek You and be a doer of Your word and ways in my life. Amen.

WITH ABILITY COMES RESPONSIBILITY

66 "Whenever God gives you a responsibility, He also gives
you the ability to meet that responsibility."

— DR. MYLES MUNROE

*"Make a careful exploration of who you are and the work you
have been given, and then sink yourself into that. Don't be
impressed with yourself. Don't compare yourself with others.
Each of you must take responsibility for doing the creative
best you can with your own life."*

— GALATIANS 6:4-5 MSG

It's amazing how time spent with doing what you were gifted to do
goes so much more peacefully. Even in storms, you find confidence
in the fact that you are at the exact place and moment in your calling.
"Careful exploration" and "work you have been given" are two phrases I
want to emphasize. Time is consistent because it is simply a measure of
the movement of earth in relation to the moon and sun (yes, way
oversimplified.) We use cosmic impacts to measure time on atomic
clocks. Your internal clock ticks based on your own internal bent and

the Heavenly purpose you were called to accomplish. You are made by and in the image of One who is infinite and impossible to know apart from His own willingness to make "THE WAY." In this relationship, internal time can be in sync. When you make a "careful exploration" of who you are and why you are made, you can start working toward figuring out the more detailed daily challenges of life with an appropriate "end in mind." The second phrase of "work you've been given" is not necessarily just a job. Work is a good thing no matter where it occurs. Labor is considered a good thing. "Let a man labor... those who work among you..." The Bible is clear that our work matters. The way it matters the most and serves its purpose is based on how we do it. We must complete it with careful exploration and avoid comparing ourselves to others. Do what you are led to do and do it well. Who you decide to be is who you will become. The careful exploration should lead you to your Creator and Father so you have access to the help you need to fulfill the original intent for your design. You don't have to get it all right and become something defined somewhere. You have creative potential you can tap into if you consistently take time to make the careful exploration and do the "work you've been given." Your future opportunities will flow from your current faithfulness with those that are before you now. That's a whole new devotional. Today, consider giving time to "careful exploration" and take advantage of the ability to do "work you've been given" with excellence. Honor God, honor who He's made you to be, and that will serve and honor people. Your abilities matter...use them in ways that matter...

Prayer

Heavenly Father, You have entrusted me as your ambassador with gifts and abilities the world needs. Help me discover through careful exploration the calling and gifts I need in order to minister in my daily sphere of influence. Help me be faithful with the little things, those things that are another man's, and unrighteous mammon so You can progress me onto bigger things, that which is my own, and true riches. Help me use my abilities to do good! Amen.

CIRCUMSTANCES SHOULDN'T DECIDE

"People are always blaming their circumstances for who they are. I don't believe in circumstances."

— GEORGE BERNARD SHAW

"Since you have heard about Jesus and have learned the truth that comes from him, throw off your old sinful nature and your former way of life, which is corrupted by lust and deception. Instead, let the Spirit renew your thoughts and attitudes. Put on your new nature, created to be like God— truly righteous and holy."

— EPHESIANS 4:21-24 NLT

Trusting in, clinging to, and relying on something or someone demonstrates belief. Consider Shaw's quote in this context. I don't trust in circumstances to shape me. I don't rely on what happens to me to shape me. I shape myself. Paul teaches us in Ephesians the essence of proactive living and taking responsibility for our attitude and actions. We are to throw off the old nature and our former way of living because it's flawed. It's corrupted by lust and the deceptive nature of sin. Sin and corruption promise a quick reward, but only gives temporary pleasure (sometimes) at the cost of great disruption to your purpose's flow. Paul says in this version, "Let the Spirit renew your thoughts and attitudes." Jesus tells us in John 6:63 His Words are Spirit. When we renew our thinking with His Word, we are essentially carrying out this truth. Philippians tells us to "let this mind be in you which was in Christ..." who humbled Himself to do what the Father asked of Him (Philippians 2:5 KJV.) Are we willing to put aside the selfishness of immediate pleasure to work toward purposeful living in the context of what the truth of the Word says? Circumstances are simply minor obstacles; continue focusing on the clear horizon of obedience that leads to purposeful living. If we struggle with vision, simply strive to be obedient to what you know. Consider who you are Spirit, Soul, and Body and work on improving in each area little by little. Take charge and let your mind's renewal and your attitude's adjustment set you apart (holy) for right living. You can't do it without Holy Spirit's help, but you can do all things through Christ who strengthens you. Bow up and decide where you are today is not where you will be tomorrow. Just like working out or running, you may experience soreness after you push yourself beyond your comfort zone, but the result of recovery is a stronger you. Do that in each domain and watch yourself grow into a powerful overcomer of circumstances. Situations may try to get you to circumvent your purpose, but you use them to train yourself into the obedience of His voice. Block out the noise daily and listen to the Holy Spirit as you renew your thoughts and attitudes to the new nature. The renewed you matters...do the work to matter...

Prayer

Heavenly Father, circumstances may try to govern me today. I ask for your help in renewing my mind, body, and spirit with Your Word so I am able to be an obedient doer and change my circumstances by changing myself. Help me to influence myself first so I may be the influencer in this world You have called me to be a disciple of truth. Come Holy Spirit and have your way in me. Reveal the truth I need as my source to obey You. Forgive me for my failures and lead me in the right paths for Your Name's sake. Amen.

DON'T FEEL TO DO, WILL TO DO!

"Action seems to follow feeling, but really action and feeling go together; and by regulating the action, which is under more direct control of the will, we can indirectly regulate the feeling, which is not."

— WILLIAM JAMES OF HARVARD

"Slowness to anger makes for deep understanding; a quick-tempered person stockpiles stupidity. A sound mind makes for a robust body, but runaway emotions corrode the bones."

— PROVERBS 14:29-30 MSG

"Moderation is better than muscle, self-control better than political power."

— PROVERBS 16:32 MSG

"Those who think they can do it on their own end up obsessed with measuring their own moral muscle but never get around to exercising it in real life. Those who trust God's

action in them find that God's Spirit is in them—living and breathing God! Obsession with self in these matters is a dead end; attention to God leads us out into the open, into a spacious, free life."

— ROMANS 8:5-6 MSG

Balance is found in disciplining self and dealing with the rabid emotions that try to lead when our will really needs to be conditioned by God's voice. The balance in realizing what you do or put into action really can "indirectly regulate the feelings." When "feeling" bad, do something. The more you "do something" (especially if it's the right thing) the more you feel good about movement. Even when movement is in the wrong direction, that is an easier mobilization than sitting still. Coaching baseball, I always teach movement in preparation for fielding a ball in the infield and outfield. "Creeping" is a strategy to get an athlete moving so motion can be adjusted to the path of the ball rather than sitting back and letting "the ball play you." We get to control our actions and that does impact our feelings. However, we have to be careful to consider Romans 8:5 and not think we rule our lives without the aid of our Helper. The Holy Spirit wants to influence our leadership of self-control, self-discipline, and choices of the will linking to our submission to God's will, servant leadership, and humility. The key to balance is to start every day seeking God's will and purpose in your life. Renew your mind to think more and more like God requires (Romans 12:1-2.) Moderation and self-control are a myth if we don't have help. James teaches us "the tongue, no man can tame (James 3:8 KJV.)" We need help to be the best version of ourselves, but God will not remove our power to choose because he gives us responsibility to control our areas of influence in a way that honors His creation (of which we are the prize, the chief, the crown.) Jesus came so He could demonstrate how to live as he prayed to the Father, "Nevertheless, not my will but thine be done." Get out and get moving, but first, make sure you are synced with all the updates available to accomplish your mission. God will order your steps if you keep your heart right and be a doer of His

Word. Get moving and be blessed. Your moderation and movement matters...do what matters...

Prayer

Heavenly Father, I ask for forgiveness in areas where I allow my emotions and evil desires to overtake my will and the obedience You expect. Let the love in my heart be reflected in my choice to obey and listen to Your voice. Holy Spirit, come and have your way in my thoughts and actions today so my moderation is a testimony to others. I desire to produce good fruit. I ask that Your kingdom comes and Your will is done. Just as Jesus prayed in the most intense prayer ever recorded in the Garden of Gethsemane, "Not my will but thine be done!" Amen.

SOW A THOUGHT, REAP AN ACTION

"The outer conditions of a person's life will always be
found to reflect their inner beliefs."

— JAMES ALLEN

*"Do not be deceived, God is not mocked; for whatever a man
sows, that he will also reap. For he who sows to his flesh will
of the flesh reap corruption, but he who sows to the Spirit
will of the Spirit reap everlasting life. And let us not grow
weary while doing good, for in due season we shall reap if we
do not lose heart. Therefore, as we have opportunity, let us do
good to all, especially to those who are of the household of
faith."*

— GALATIANS 6:7-10 NKJV

This quote is so true and the Word of God is clear we reap what
we sow. We have to learn to simplify our life's motives and
understandings to ensure the fruit of what we do truly matches our
intent. On my wall at work is a reworded summary from a quote by
Ralph Waldo Emerson that reads, "Be careful what you think...Your

thoughts become your words...your words become your actions...your actions become your habits...your habits become your character...your character becomes your destiny." Emerson had the original idea, but the author of this follow up quote is unknown. Sowing and reaping applies to our thoughts, actions, habits, character, and destiny (destination.) You go where you think, speak, and develop yourself to go. You must simplify the vision and the outcomes you are driven toward by focusing on what you know God has called you to do and how you are called to do it. Dedicate yourself to be a finisher and take responsibility to walk in integrity around the authenticity of who you are and how that relates to what you do. You are not the job you do, but the way you do the job demonstrates who you are. Be a person of authenticity, discipline, and diligence. God bless you as you slow down the processes going on around you to prioritize the "Big Rocks" as Stephen Covey would say. Put First Things First and make sure you are digging deep into your personal ethos to establish with clarity what those "big rocks" are. YouTube has a great video of the "big rocks" demonstration Stephen Covey did at a 7 Habits training years ago. This idea of "big rocks" is a great metaphor for prioritization and purpose. Work on the inner conditions to ensure the outer fruit reflects your inner beauty. Be blessed as you obey! Your thoughts and priorities matter...Do what matters...

Prayer

Heavenly Father, I give you praise and thanks for all that You have blessed me with in life. I ask for help in being a good steward of my thoughts, words, and actions so my character reflects the fruit of the Spirit and leads me to the right destination. I am grateful for Holy Spirit influence in my life and ask for clarity to prioritize and align my "big rocks" with Yours. Come Holy Spirit and influence my life in such a way that my discipleship reflects the right teaching and execution. Holy Spirit, light my Spirit as your candle so I can be the light in this world I am called to be. Amen.

FAITHFULNESS: GOD'S PLUMB LINE

"Well done is better than well said."

— BENJAMIN FRANKLIN

"His lord said unto him, Well done, thou good and faithful servant: thou hast been faithful over a few things, I will make thee ruler over many things: enter thou into the joy of thy lord."

— MATTHEW 25:21 KJV

"He that is faithful in that which is least is faithful also in much: and he that is unjust in the least is unjust also in much. If therefore ye have not been faithful in the unrighteous mammon, who will commit to your trust the true riches? And if ye have not been faithful in that which is another man's, who shall give you that which is your own? No servant can serve two masters: for either he will hate the one, and love the other; or else he will hold to the one, and despise the other. Ye cannot serve God and mammon."

— LUKE 16:10-13 KJV

The passages of scripture here both represent faithful stewardship. The scripture in Matthew is repeatedly similar to each of the stewards who was faithful to increase the value of the talents or sum of money entrusted (parable of the talents) to him. The trustee who buried the talent was scolded and out of relationship with the master. The implication I gain is we are entrusted with gifts and talents we must utilize in order to grow our worth and the worth of those we serve. When one proves faithful, they see growth in the trust and resources of the master.

The passage in Luke teaches us there are three things we are required to be faithful stewards of:

1. That which is least or the little things.
2. Unrighteous mammon – material wealth.
3. That which is another man's. Faithfulness in the "little things" causes" causes us to be rewarded with more or bigger things. Faithfulness in unrighteous mammon qualifies us to receive "true riches," and faithfulness in that which is another man's gives us the right to have that which is our own.

In daily life, we are to steward or take responsibility for the little things. The way we handle the little details reveals how we will handle the bigger details. Do the little things first and you will see bigger opportunities arise. You must crawl before you walk. You must earn your first hundred before you earn your first thousand. Progressions that don't match this model will probably land you in confusion and mismanagement. As you honor God and prove faithful by being a generous giver and tither, God can trust you with kingdom wealth, which far surpasses money. Love of money is the root of all evil, but your use of money can prove valuable in His kingdom purposes for your life. You rule the money while being ruled by God and He will be able to trust you with spiritual gifts. Ever wonder why someone else has a big successful business? They were probably faithful with another man's business. How many small entrepreneur ventures were started from individuals sowing years into another opportunity to find they could work for themselves and provide a similar service at a value while still making a profit? I believe these three points of faithfulness are entry points into next levels of reward from our Father who loves us and wants us to prosper and be in health even as our soul prospers. Be faithful. It's God's plumb line. Faithful stewardship demonstrates the walls are square for God to furnish the house of your life. You matter... your faithfulness matters...do what matters...

Prayer

Heavenly Father, I desire to be a good and faithful servant. Help me to steward the gifts and talents that You have placed within my life. I know every good and perfect gift comes from above and I desire to use all of that good to be a faithful steward. Holy Spirit come fill me with the wisdom and life fruit to be a doer of the good works You have called me to do. I want to hear my Father say, WELL DONE! Amen.

LOOK UP, LOOK DOWN, AND RUN YOUR RACE

"Look up to the sky. You'll never find rainbows if you're looking down."

— CHARLIE CHAPLAIN

"Know ye not that they which run in a race run all, but one receiveth the prize? So run, that ye may obtain. And every man that striveth for the mastery is temperate in all things. Now they do it to obtain a corruptible crown; but we an incorruptible. I therefore so run, not as uncertainly; so fight I, not as one that beateth the air: But I keep under my body, and bring it into subjection: lest that by any means, when I have preached to others, I myself should be a castaway."

— I CORINTHIANS 9:24-27 KJV

Looking up is a brilliant idea in my mind. As Mr. Chaplain said, looking down can cause you to miss the rainbow and many other beautiful things. This is metaphorically a good idea as well. We often use the phrase "look up" to express this idea of a vision of hope and grander things. When we are looking down at the grind, we sometimes miss the "big picture." I think there are times; however, when we do need to look down as well. A while back, I was running at Berry College up this mountain road that leads to a reservoir. On my right was the beautiful mountain incline and on my left was this placid lake of beautiful water. As I rounded a bend, I began to climb up the mountain road, leaving the beautiful water behind me. I remember that I looked up and could not see the peak of the hill I was to climb. Having run this many times before, I knew the climb was less than a mile but more than half. I decided I wanted to run up the entire hill and not relent to walking as I have so many times. Due to the steep grade and the hopeless view with no end in sight, I chose to look down at the ground. I focused on my feet, taking this challenge one step at a time. Breaking down this task into short, slow jogging steps allowed me to reach the top without walking. This life lesson is a simple, yet profound one. When hopelessness creeps into life, sometimes you can benefit from looking down and just taking on the challenge one step at a time. Paul exhorts the Corinthian church that this life is like a race that we run and we are running with the intent to obtain the prize. We must discipline our bodies and make it be subject to the training and effort required to win. This is an appropriate way to look at life's challenges. It's a race many run, but only one receives the prize. Run in such a way that the prize is attainable so you don't waste your life. Look up to see the big picture in the beauty all around, look down to see the next steps in the grind and do the little things that will get you there. Discipline yourself to ensure your body, mind, and spirit are aligned to the mission so you may obtain the prize. Run to win. You matter...do what matters...

Prayer

Heavenly Father, I am grateful for the beauty of Your creation. I am thankful for the promise represented in the rainbow. I am most appreciative of the grace afforded to me by Your Son and the work of the Cross which gives me access to the life I need to run my race with confidence and conviction. Help me to run well in the race that is before me and to look up to Jesus, the author and finisher of my faith. Help me to submit humbly to the daily faithfulness necessary to accomplish my purpose and be with me as I run to obtain the crown of life that is promised to those who call upon Your name. Come Holy Spirit and have your way in my life. Amen.

STAND LIKE A ROCK

> "In matters of style, swim with the current, on matters of principle stand like a rock."
>
> — THOMAS JEFFERSON

> *"Wisdom is the principal thing; therefore get wisdom: and with all thy getting get understanding."*
>
> — PROVERBS 4:7 KJV

> *"The fear of the Lord is the beginning of wisdom: and the knowledge of the holy is understanding."*
>
> — PROVERBS 9:10 KJV

Wisdom is the principal thing and it leads to principles that should lead us. The fear of God is the beginning of wisdom. The house that was built upon the rock was built upon obeying God's Word. Jesus said a wise man builds his house upon the rock and the winds and rains (storms of life) cannot destroy it. What are you filling your mind with today? Is it sandy style or rocky principles? I will identify one principle we could all hang our hat on during these troubling times. Love the Lord your God with all your heart, soul, mind and strength and your neighbor as yourself. Love never fails. Love does not seek its own. Love endures. Check out 1 Corinthians 13. We can get overwhelmed with the realities that stress us and all the tantalizing coverage of man's ideas, but what will stand is the Word and what God said. It doesn't really matter in eternity what everyone else's style is or their opinion. What matters is Christ, Him crucified, and his principles of wisdom on living. Get on solid ground of the word and don't be moved by the currents of opinion, strife, contention, and murder. Having done all to stand, stand in the full armor of God. Be blessed as you stand on God's principles, respecting and honoring His wisdom. You matter...do what matters...

Prayer

Heavenly Father, I come to You with a humble heart and ask that You reveal to me the trends and styles that do not align with Your principles. Help me to owe no man anything but to love him. You have put your love in my heart so I can avoid sinning against You. Help me as I seek to stand on Your word. I expect persecution to come for the Word's sake. I need Your Spirit in me to withstand the doubts and fears that would cause me to sway and stumble. Help me to remain strong and avoid the double-mindedness that causes the ship of my life to be tossed by winds and waves. Come Holy Spirit and make yourself unto me wisdom. Amen.

NO FEAR

"Of all the liars in the world, sometimes the worst are our own fears."

— RUDYARD KIPLING

"For God hath not given us the spirit of fear; but of power, and of love, and of a sound mind."

— 2 TIMOTHY 1:7 KJV

"For in Jesus Christ neither circumcision availeth anything, nor uncircumcision; but faith which worketh by love."

— GALATIANS 5:6 KJV

"And now abideth faith, hope, charity, these three; but the greatest of these is charity.'

— 1 CORINTHIANS 13:13 KJV

During the Rocky IV movie, there is this scene in Rocky's corner where his trainer is speaking affirmations to get his mindset right and he's saying, "No fear, no pain, no fear, no pain." There was potential for fear because the fighter had already killed Apollo. This movie was so powerful on so many levels. It dealt with race, patriotism, empathy, and "no fear." Faith vs. Fear. Fear is a spiritual force, not a feeling. Being scared is a feeling. Happiness is to Joy as Scared is to Fear. Happiness may be a by-product of joy, but joy is fruit of spiritual life in you. Being afraid is a by-product of fear not given by God, but we overcome this fear and its fruits by power, love, and the soundness of mind we inherit through His grace. Faith is the spiritual force giving us access to this power, love, and soundness of mind. Fear gives us access to double-minded cowardly instability, division, and worry. When fear creeps in and feeds you, it is building up the confidence in an outcome that is not aligned with God's best and your desires. Fear torments us into anxiety and negative expectations. Faith encourages us to press through because there is an earnest expectation everything is working to my good. Even if it's not shaping up for my good, my God's purposes are being manifested and He is good. Faith feeds on the truth of His Word. Faith gets into the fight and is a "doer." Walk by faith, believing that God is God and He is a Rewarder of those who diligently seek Him. Love God, Love yourself, and Love His people (all people.) "No fear" is not a cheap slogan. It is the closing of a door to destruction that needs to be closed. Don't forget to be sure to add faith. Faith works by love. With all that's going one, don't fear speaking up for love, empathy, and unity. Don't let fear close your ears to listening. Don't let fear raise anxiety so logical thought and actions (sound mind) can't prevail. Don't give energy to the hatred of people you don't even know. Remember, faith worketh by love. Faith is a spiritual force. It's impossible to please God without it. Perfect LOVE casts out FEAR. Our world is full of fear. The answer is FAITH, HOPE, and LOVE (charity.) Greatest is love because it fuels the other. Love caused Jesus to afford us the grace we need and the measure of faith that saves. Be blessed with POWER, LOVE, and a SOUND MIND! NO FEAR! You matter...do what matters...

. . .

Prayer

Heavenly Father, I stand against the power of fear. Your Word says that fear has torment and You have not given me a spirit of fear but of power, love, and a sound mind. Help me to live at peace in my mind and overcome the lies of fear that try to distract me from Godly pursuits. Come Holy Spirit and assist my love walk and my faith walk so I demonstrate power, love, and soundness of mind and heart. Amen.

FAITHFUL DOERS

"Let us have faith that right makes might, and that faith, let us, to the end, dare to do our duty as we understand it."

— ABRAHAM LINCOLN

"If your faith remains strong, even while surrounded by life's difficulties, you will continue to experience the untold blessings of God! True happiness comes as you pass the test with faith, and receive the victorious crown of life promised to every lover of God."

— JAMES 1:12 TPT

"After this manner therefore pray ye: Our Father which art in heaven, Hallowed be thy name. Thy kingdom come. Thy will be done on earth, as it is in heaven. Give us this day our daily bread. And forgive us our debts, as we forgive our debtors. And lead us not into temptation, but deliver us from evil: for thine is the kingdom, and the power, and the glory, for ever. Amen."

— MATTHEW 6: 9-13 KJV

P resident Lincoln was certainly faced with many challenges and tests of will and faith. He encourages in this quote that our faith should lead us into a "right makes might" scenario. What do you and I believe? Does what we believe and put our faith in align with what is right so God is able to back us? Do we dare to do our duty as we see what our Heavenly Father commands? Faith is the substance of things hoped for and it comes by hearing God's Word. Hearing alone isn't enough. We must dare to become doers. Obedience is our demonstration we trust our Father and desire to please Him. We are saved by grace (not our works) through faith (not just believing, but believing truth.) Strong faith while being surrounded by the challenges of life that test us is Paul's encouragement here. Life's difficulties, peoples' negative influences, failures and struggles are not the final prize. We run to the promise He purchased eternal life for us. We are told the end result of endurance through testing is the crown of life. In the weight room, muscles are challenged and they grow most when they are worked to failure. The greatest growth in muscle occurs when the muscle is stretched beyond its current comfort. The muscle responds with adaptations causing it to get bigger and more efficient so the training effect leads to a better chance of success on future lifts with heavier weight. In life, our challenges that stretch us beyond comfort help us to grow and get stronger. "Our Father who art in heaven, hallowed be thy name..." He is our King and the King. We are His people, the sheep of His pasture, and we hear His voice. "Thy kingdom come, thy will be done in earth as it is in heaven," (Matthew 6: 9-10 KJV.) May we be obedient to His word so we serve as ambassadors in earth and bring His kingdom purposes into fruition in this life through His grace and power. "Give us this day our daily bread..." His provision came in a variety of ways, but ultimately, Jesus and Paul taught us to work and trust. Do what you know to do and trust God to bless and provide more than enough so you can be a blessing to others. "Forgive us our trespasses as we forgive those who trespass against us." This one is big. Our Savior has provided forgiveness far beyond our comprehension because we don't even know all that is forgiven daily by our Father. May we humble ourselves under His grace. Find truth in His Word and not get entangled in thought contrary to His truth. Love God, love yourself, and love your neighbor. Such is the Gospel of Christ's message to us. The enemy is seeking to destroy God's creation, but the Savior is capable of redeeming all that is lost and is not seeking to destroy, but to save. Be saved, live saved, and repent quickly when faith gets distracted by fear. Be a faithful doer of what you know you should and trust God to bless you. You matter...be a doer of what matters...

Prayer

Heavenly Father, I come to you with a humble heart and hungry spirit. I desire to endure and pass all of life's tests and challenges to obtain the crown of life. Help me to be a faithful doer of your guiding principles. Come Holy Spirit and have your way in my life, in my choices, in my results. In Jesus' mighty name, I commit to being a faithful doer of all that is commanded. Lead me and guide me into all truth. Amen.

BEYOND FINGER PAINTING:
PLAY BALL

"How many observe Christ's birthday! How few, His precepts!"

— BENJAMIN FRANKLIN

"So come on, let's leave the preschool finger painting exercises on Christ and get on with the grand work of art. Grow up in Christ. The basic foundational truths are in place: turning your back on "salvation by self-help" and turning in trust toward God; baptismal instructions; laying on of hands; resurrection of the dead; eternal judgment. God helping us, we'll stay true to all that. But there's so much more. Let's get on with it."

— HEBREWS 6:1-3 MSG

I remember the years of coaching baseball when my boys were playing. You could use practice drills to teach kids how to hit without them even realizing they were learning every part of the swing. I remember hearing coaches, dads, etc., yelling the same types of cues (keep your head on the ball, eye on the ball, hands inside the ball, hips and hands....) These cues are supposed to give a quick memory jar and increase the chances the batter adjusts and makes contact. It's time for us, as Believers, to leave the fundamental "finger painting" where we keep our head on the ball and swing correctly moving onto the more complex tasks of the game. It's time for us to step into the game with confidence and break the game open because we know so much more than just the fundamentals. We have to live the fundamentals and live right, but we also need to leave the "salvation by self-help" and trust God to lead us into much greater places where His influence causes us to explore greater aspects of creation than just the basics. The basics are awesome and critical, but it's time for us to play "travel ball" or at least make it to the All Stars. Dig in and be diligent to demonstrate faithfulness while expanding your territory by reaching out to discover more of His plan for your life. How are we to discover what's "so much more?" Dig deep into meditating on His word (Joshua 1:8), be a faithful doer of what you know, and pray without ceasing. Try to involve His will and expect Him to do exceedingly, abundantly more than you could ask or think. Learn the principles and precepts of right living and execute the fundamentals consistently while growing into a more elite player. Let's play ball!

Prayer

Heavenly Father, I'm ready to "play ball" and get into Your game. I pray that you reveal to me what I need to do to become the living sacrifice You expect. Help me to move past elementary tasks of my faith walk and grow to receive the meat of the word so I can grow thereby. Come Holy Spirit and inspire my heart with Your breath, Your ideas, and Your power. I submit my will to Yours and commit to becoming the mature person of God You have called me to be. Amen.

3 FOOT WORLD

"Only focus on your three-foot world," he said. "Focus on what you can affect. You keep looking around, and none of that can help you right now, can it?"

— MARK OWEN IN *NO HERO: THE EVOLUTION OF A NAVY SEAL*

"Don't fret or worry. Instead of worrying, pray. Let petitions and praises shape your worries into prayers, letting God know your concerns. Before you know it, a sense of God's wholeness, everything coming together for good, will come and settle you down. It's wonderful what happens when Christ displaces worry at the center of your life."

— PHILIPPIANS 4:6-7 MSG

"If you decide for God, living a life of God-worship, it follows that you don't fuss about what's on the table at mealtimes or whether the clothes in your closet are in fashion. There is far more to your life than the food you put in your stomach, more to your outer appearance than the clothes you hang on your

*body. Look at the birds, free and unfettered, not tied down to
a job description, careless in the care of God. And you count
far more to him than birds."*

— MATTHEW 6:25-26 MSG

In his book *No Hero: The Evolution of a Navy SEAL*, Mark Owen talks about fear using a metaphor in climbing he called "the three-foot world." He was paralyzed by his fear of heights when climbing with an instructor on a fairly complicated rock face. He was over using anchors for his line (I know very little about climbing) and the instructor who was "free climbing" (no safety harnesses or ropes) came behind him and was taking out every other one so he would have them, as needed. This instructor talked to Mark about simply living in his 3 Foot World and only worrying about a single foot, one hand placement at a time. He would only reach the top by living in his 3 Foot World. Sometimes we can benefit from looking back and celebrating a good memory or rejoicing over a past victory and it is important to have vision for our future and plan ahead; however, when fear and anxiety try to paralyze movement and keep us still, we must remember these passages:

1. Don't worry or fret
2. Do pray and
3. Remember the birds.

Worrying and fretting just increase paralysis while trusting and praying welcome Another (Our comforter and friend, Holy Spirit) onto the scene to help in your 3 Foot World. Remember prayer is your invitation to God to come interact with heavenly influence in your domain..."thy kingdom come, thy will be done..." We can look at nature and see birds and flowers are taken care of by the Father. He cares much more for us. Jesus said that. God is with you and He will not forsake you so, don't fret and worry, just pray and remember God loves you more than a bird. Be blessed and at peace. Work daily with confidence there is a helper with you. Stay in your three foot world with the Helper that's out of this world. You matter...do what matters...

. . .

Prayer

Heavenly Father, I praise your powerful name and ask that Your Kingdom come and Your will be done in my 3 Foot World. Help me to overcome fear and distractions while climbing to the heights that You designate for me to climb. I know that Your Word is the anchor and patience is the rope that will lead me into the safe spaces on my journey toward the peak. Come Holy Spirit and join me in my climb. Help me to be strong and courageous as I ascend. Amen.

PRINCIPLE AND POWER OF PRIORITIES

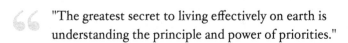

"The greatest secret to living effectively on earth is understanding the principle and power of priorities."

— DR. MYLES MUNROE

"But seek ye first the kingdom of God, and his righteousness; and all these things shall be added unto you."

— MATTHEW 6:33 KJV

"Good friend, take to heart what I'm telling you; collect my counsels and guard them with your life. Tune your ears to the world of Wisdom; set your heart on a life of Understanding. That's right—if you make Insight your priority, and won't take no for an answer, Searching for it like a prospector panning for gold, like an adventurer on a treasure hunt, Believe me, before you know it Fear-of- God will be yours; you'll have come upon the Knowledge of God."

— PROVERBS 2:1-5 MSG

Priorities are important. That's the essence of the word, huh? Be sure to prioritize insight. We should seek to examine how things really are and what is most important. The Word encourages the priority of the Kingdom. Proverbs teaches us to get wisdom and get understanding. There is also a practical side that can get overlooked. We can read the Word and gain understanding, but not utilize the understanding because we let the less important things push us away from our priorities. Just because something is good or okay doesn't mean it should be a priority. Focus on priority relationships first. Schedule your day where you invest in tasks that enhance people and the relationships in your life that push you toward your goals. Take some time each day to plan and schedule the priorities. If you don't, circumstances you can't control will creep in and distract you from what you can control. Live by design, not default. Schedule time in your day to consider what the most important tasks and "to do" list items are and be intentional. Make sure the investment of those "to do" lists leads to better relationships and growth opportunities with the most important people in your life. You are the programmer of your life. Write the program to live intentionally. Never let the things that matter most take a back seat to those that matter least. Don't let the people who matter most feel as they don't. If your relationship with God is a priority, you must intentionally give time and energy to it. If your relationship with your spouse matters, you must intentionally give time to improve it. If your kids matter you must intentionally invest in those relationships. If your job/vocation matters, you must invest in giving it your best energy and focus when you are there. Be intentional with your time and you will be intentional with your life and you will find more and more success and fulfillment. Your priorities matter... You matter... do what matters.

Prayer

Heavenly Father, You are the King of kings and Lord of lords. There is no one like You. You are the priority relationship in my life. Help me to love You with all of my heart, soul, mind and strength and my neighbor as myself. Holy Spirit, come and help me to prioritize my day so my efforts in all that I do produce good fruits for You. I will seek first the Kingdom of God and His righteousness with the expectation that obedience to seek first will result in all my other concerns and needs being met beyond what I could ask or think. Amen.

SELF-AWARE: THINK ABOUT THINKING

"We are self-aware. This awareness means that we can stand mentally outside of ourselves and evaluate our beliefs and our actions. We can think about what we think."

— STEPHEN R. COVEY

"A sound mind makes for a robust body, but runaway emotions corrode the bones."

— PROVERBS 14:30 MSG

"For God hath not given us the spirit of fear; but of power, and of love, and of a sound mind."

— 2 TIMOTHY 1:7 KJV

"And do not be conformed to this world [any longer with its superficial values and customs], but be transformed and progressively changed [as you mature spiritually] by the renewing of your mind [focusing on godly values and ethical

*attitudes], so that you may prove [for yourselves] what the
will of God is, that which is good and acceptable and perfect
[in His plan and purpose for you]."*

— ROMANS 12:2 AMPLIFIED

I n the education world, we talk about metacognition. This basically
is thinking about how you think. What an awesome idea. We often
hear phrases like "knowledge is power" and "a mind is a terrible thing
to waste." Time is also a terrible thing to waste, but we often rush and
hustle in ways that inefficiently use time in activities that are
counterproductive to our best efforts. Pause....
Really...pause...reflect...or as Psalms would say, "Selah," meaning "pause
and think about this." As we pause and think about how we think, we
know that "as a man thinketh in his heart, so is he." Proverbs doesn't
say as a man thinks, so is he. It requires thinking with the brain and
with the "self-aware" portions of our heart. We must engage in
intentional, meaningful thought and be governed by principles of the
Word if we want our thought life to produce fruit moving forward. You
can produce good fruits consistently without nourishing the roots and
our lives are rooted in our thought life. My encouragement today is to
intentionally take some precious time to consider your thought life.
Think about how you are thinking and how you are talking because
that is the root of the issues that come forth out of your life. You have
the power to choose...not only your actions, but you get to govern your
own thought life. You can't control every thought that enters, but you
can choose to coordinate thoughts and discipline your mind so it is
renewed to paradigms that are for your good and your growth. You can
set aside brief moments every day to design your own "mind gym" and
work your mind the way you want. Exercise your thought life
intentionally through meditation, gratitude, and memorization. I often
memorize quotes and scriptures to assist me with keeping positive
mental thoughts at the forefront of my thinking. May our thoughts be
governed by values and principles that God reveals so our purpose and
passion align with His principles and His plan. How? Read Joshua 1:8,
Proverbs 4:20-25, and John 1:1; 6:63 in addition to the scriptures given

with this devotion. Learn to meditate (mutter back and memorize) the Word of God as it is life, health, substance, and truth. We are all looking for truth, and the Truth. Well, when we've found Jesus, we've found the Way, the Truth, and the Life. Your thoughts matter. You matter...do what matters.

Prayer

Heavenly Father, I recognize the importance of my thought life and that it is governed by the truth of your word. I desire to take captive every thought and make my thoughts subject to your governing authority. Help me to meditate on your word and think right about all truth that is shared with me. Come Holy Spirit and renew my mind daily by Your influence and the influence of the WORD! Amen.

DILIGENTLY SEEK HIM

> "God gives every bird his worm, but he does not throw it into the nest."

— SWEDISH PROVERB

> *"By faith Enoch was taken away so that he did not see death,*
> *"and was not found, because God had taken him"; for before*
> *he was taken he had this testimony, that he pleased God. But*
> *without faith it is impossible to please Him, for he who*
> *comes to God must believe that He is, and that He is a*
> *rewarder of those who diligently seek Him."*

— HEBREWS 11:5-6 NKJV

We often excuse our inactivity with "waiting on God." We blame so much of life on circumstances out of our control and do very little to consider how we might impact every moment of our life. We focus on one aspect or one instance in our life rather than looking at ways we can consistently impact our daily improvement. When I get frustrated with what I cannot impact, the best way to change the outlook is when I just choose to impact something I can.

God is a faith God. He expects us to expect Him to be active and powerful in our lives, but we tend to tiptoe around what we claim to believe. God rewards those who "diligently" seek Him. Diligence and tenacity cause us to get after things without reserve. Wisdom is important and there are times for stillness, but don't sit around waiting for something special to happen. Be someone special that makes things happen. May we be those who believe God is all powerful, an ever present help, and a rewarder of my pursuit. May we be in "hot pursuit." Diligently seek Him. The Bible says that, if we seek Him, we will find Him. That's just the truth. Diligently seek Him and your finding of Him will uncover a lot more than you could imagine, and the pursuit will distract you from the many frustrations that tend to distract. Be blessed as you believe and pursue. You matter...do what matters...

Prayer

Heavenly Father, I come to you and thank You for Your consistent presence in my life. I desire to have a testimony like Enoch where it can be said that I walk with God. When my life is over, I desire to have been one who diligently sought after truth and obedience to my Father's plan. God help me to be attentive to the details of my life and obedient to the prompting of the Holy Spirit as I pursue a life of meaning and relevance in this world. Help me to be in the world but not of this world. Come Holy Spirit and have Your way in my life. Do what is pleasing to You and my days will be blessed. Amen.

TRIAL BY FIRE

> "If you can't stand the heat, get out of the kitchen."
>
> — HARRY S. TRUMAN

> *"Everyone's going through a refining fire sooner or later, but you'll be well-preserved, protected from the eternal flames. Be preservatives yourselves. Preserve the peace."*
>
> — MARK 9:49-50 MSG

> *"For every one shall be salted with fire, and every sacrifice shall be salted with salt. Salt is good: but if the salt have lost his saltness, wherewith will ye season it? Have salt in yourselves, and have peace one with another."*
>
> — MARK 9:49-50 KJV

Even in our air-conditioned house and well-insulated oven, when Amy gets that big meal going, the kitchen gets hotter, but that's where the action is and she can't just leave her food to chance. She's gotta stay with it to enjoy the awesome end result. My eldest son Caleb went through the fire at age 15. He was working really hard to get bigger and stronger in his pursuit to play baseball. He was going to workouts in the morning and then working out again during the weight training class he had scheduled. He had really grown in his stature, but his muscles seemed to stop growing. He got his wisdom teeth pulled over the summer of his sophomore year and a couple of weeks after the surgery, he got sick and couldn't keep food down all weekend. A similar episode began happening every 8-10 days with intense stomach cramps and vomiting. We went to doctors, specialists, a chiropractor, and the alter trying to seek answers. He went from around 120 pounds to 80 pounds from August to October and looked like a starving child in a third world country. I remember sitting on the couch with him and praying for him while I'd put my hand on his belly. We finally got the answers we were looking for and found he had a blockage in his intestines. This was a fire that taught us so much about how to stand together, pray, trust, and seek the right kind of help. Caleb is healthy and strong following a surgery and takes a medicine to help his intestines from getting inflamed. After the surgery, he immediately recovered and began getting stronger.

During this "furnace of adversity" (phrase often used by my dear friend Chadd Wright), Amy found a scripture in the Old Testament about three Jewish men who were thrown in a fiery furnace for their loyalty to God's law. They came out of that furnace without the smell of smoke. The analogy of refining with fire, or potter's wheel, etc. can be a very interesting one with the human condition. I read this scripture over and over about cutting off parts of your body that tempt you so you don't end up in hell. After those admonishments from Jesus, we get this passage. In life, the heat is on. Satan roams trying to kill, steal, and destroy, but Jesus has given us access to life because He came to give life and that more abundantly. The fire seems to be a causation of saltiness in Mark 9. When the fire comes, will it produce salt in you that preserves you from the stench and pain of the flames or will you lose your saltiness through fear and doubt and be overcome with the flames so that, rather than purity and saltiness, they produce bitterness, unbelief, and fear? Fire happens. It's called life, but "be of good cheer, I have overcome the world ," (John 16:33 KJV.) Faithful living produces a salty life saving you and others from the pain of getting burned. Experiences of overcoming the furnace produce patient endurance which produces great reward (James 1.) Many times the "consuming fire" appeared and did not consume. Let the flame of the Holy Spirit be present and make a salt factory in your life. You'll come out without the smell of smoke and with a testimony of excellence that can help others. Be salty not charred. You matter...do what matters...

Prayer

Heavenly Father, help me stand in the face of difficult challenges and furnaces of adversity on faith in the Son of God who gave of Himself so I can become salty. I desire to represent you well. Help me to never grow weary in well-doing knowing that I will reap if I don't faint. Come Holy Spirit and help me to stand up for what is right and allow You to be the Potter as You make me the vessel of Your love that You desire. Thank You for working in me to make me complete in You and confident in the outcome that will always work to my good. Amen.

PRICE OF SPARROWS: KNOW YOUR WORTH

> The brain said, "I'm the smartest organ in the body." The heart said, "Who told you?"

— STEPHEN COVEY

"What is the price of two sparrows—one copper coin? But not a single sparrow can fall to the ground without your Father knowing it. And the very hairs on your head are all numbered. So don't be afraid; you are more valuable to God than a whole flock of sparrows."

— MATTHEW 10:29-31 NLT

"The Lord is my shepherd; I have all that I need. He lets me rest in green meadows; he leads me beside peaceful streams. He renews my strength. He guides me along right paths, bringing honor to his name."

— PSALMS 23:1-3 NLT

Humans are special creatures. Human = humus (dirt) + man (spirit/ruwah.) We are a spiritual being housed in a dirt body that is composed of many of the same components as the earth. You are a special creation, though. Consider the lilies and the sparrows. They are both beautiful in how they do their thing, but they are both sustained by the hand of God. You are much more valuable to God than either lilies or sparrows. The Lord is our God and King and He knows all of creation to the very detail of DNA. He is the Creator of everything we know and so much more. He has the hair on our heads numbered. Not one sparrow can fall without the Father knowing it. "So don't be afraid, you are more valuable to God than a whole flock of sparrows." Wow...sometimes it would be good for us to simply read a scripture over and over and get it solidly into our hearts. We are valuable enough to God to be given His attention. "The Lord (the ONE GOD who is King of Kings, Creator, etc.) is MY shepherd, I have all I need (because of Him.)" (Emphasis added) My paths are His design to honor His name. Jesus commanded we love God with all of our hearts, soul, mind and strength and our neighbor as ourselves. We are to love even our enemies. Neighbors aren't chosen, they are just proximal to where you are. We are given the command to love God, love others, and by implication love ourselves. Please recognize the great value you have and remember that you are fearfully and wonderfully made and your very hairs are numbered. The omniscience of your Creator is not even challenged to know everything about you or care for you deeply. May we trust and believe we mean more to God than the birds and flowers He clothes and feeds. We are like the sheep owned by a good Shepherd. He desires our lives to be a testimony of His care for us. A good shepherd cares for His sheep and His sheep hear His voice and obey. May my ears be tuned, my heart believe, my mouth confirm and confess, and my life bring honor to His name.

Prayer

Heavenly Father, I am grateful You know me so well that even the hairs on my head are numbered. I am more valuable than flowers and birds and You take care of them. Help me to trust Your words and trust You to perform these words in me. Holy Spirit, guide me along the right paths and bring honor to Your name by the glory represented by the blessings You place in my life. Thank you for your mercy and grace to make me a vessel of honor. Amen.

LEADERSHIP IS SERVANTHOOD

"As we look ahead into the next century, leaders will be those who empower others."

— BILL GATES

"But Jesus called them to Himself and said, "You know that the rulers of the Gentiles lord it over them, and those who are great exercise authority over them. Yet it shall not be so among you; but whoever desires to become great among you, let him be your servant. And whoever desires to be first among you, let him be your slave—"just as the Son of Man did not come to be served, but to serve, and to give His life a ransom for many."

— MATHEW 20:25-28 NKJV

"But he who is greatest among you shall be your servant. And whoever exalts himself will be humbled, and he who humbles himself will be exalted."

— MATTHEW 23:11-12 NKJV

Isn't it refreshing that people all over the world recognize the importance of servant leadership. In September of 2019, I was preparing for the DRT 50K with a training run on the Duncan Ridge Trail in the North Georgia Mountains. The weekend before I was to run this race, I committed to crewing some friends who were running a 50 Miler at the Georgia Jewel. One of those competitors was unable to run so he decided to crew the other two team members in my stead and I would pivot and crew my friend, Chadd Wright. Chadd is a very strong ultra runner and overall tough dude. He had recently retired from the Navy where he had served 12 years as an active duty Navy SEAL. Chadd was running the 100 mile ultra event at the Georgia Jewel and I was tasked with crewing him in the race he hoped to win. Chadd wound up asking me with a little under 20 miles to go if I would run with him. He had already run 80 miles so I thought I might be able to keep up and be a help to him. It was dark and we ran 18.66 miles together in darkness on some pretty tough terrain in the North Georgia mountain close to Dalton, GA. Chadd came in 2nd in the race and gave me the belt buckle he earned for his outstanding performance. I certainly didn't expect anything for crewing Chadd. I did it to be a blessing to a friend and I enjoyed getting to meet some wonderful people and seeing him compete. That 18.66 miles I ran with Chadd still remains some of the most memorable mileage I've run and one of the more rewarding experiences in my life. I think I ran better because I was focused on being a servant to him rather than competing myself. Servant leadership is not a type of leadership. All good leadership is servanthood. Bill Gates is accurate in saying that "leaders will be those who empower others." All good leaders do that. Leadership is servanthood. If our Savior, Jesus himself, gives the example of servanthood as the description of His life lived on purpose, it would be wise for us to consider how we can employ that same mindset in living out our leadership journey. Lead well. Start with yourself. Make decisions you know will serve you well in becoming your best self so you can benefit others you have the opportunity to serve. The humility of servant leadership exalts the servant from the place below to a place of honor. Serve others and see how your leadership influence grows and impacts positive change. You matter...do what matters...

. . .

Prayer

Heavenly Father, help me take on the mindset Jesus had when He humbled Himself to serve us by obedience to death on the cross. Give me the strength to look to others who I can benefit and contribute to their mission. Help me empower those around me to lead themselves well and become humble servants as well. Come, Holy Spirit and order my steps so I am in the right place at the right time to be a blessing to others, empowering them to live life loud! Amen.

OBEY AND PRAY FOR GODLY AUTHORITY

"Do not pray for easy lives. Pray to be stronger men."

— JOHN F. KENNEDY

"Make the Master proud of you by being good citizens. Respect the authorities, whatever their level; they are God's emissaries for keeping order. It is God's will that by doing good, you might cure the ignorance of the fools who think you're a danger to society. Exercise your freedom by serving God, not by breaking the rules. Treat everyone you meet with dignity. Love your spiritual family. Revere God. Respect the government."

— I PETER 2:15-17 THE MESSAGE

"I exhort therefore, that, first of all, supplications, prayers, intercessions, and giving of thanks, be made for all men; For kings, and for all that are in authority; that we may lead a quiet and peaceable life in all godliness and honesty."

— I TIMOTHY 2:1-2 KJV

I t is easy to get cynical and negative about politics and leadership in general. Local, state, and national leaders are all, after all, just men and women like you and me trying to do a job. President Kennedy was looked up to as an inspiring president and one who motivated some significant change prior to his assassination. Regardless of your political bent and how you lean in terms of your interest in the United States political process, the Bible clearly teaches us we have to submit and respect the government. We are to love and respect our churches, our government, and the people in positions of authority. They are God's servants for keeping order in our society. As we see so much disorder and disarray, we have to remember God is not American. It is important we remember that, although our nation was founded on Biblical principles and many of our leaders have historically honored God, we are not living in a world where honoring God is the norm. It is important we pray, in faith, believing God will put the right men and women in authority so we can have the right kind of order. I even try to remember to pray over my money, including the tax dollars coming out of my paycheck to assist with funding the government. We have a responsibility to pray for "kings, and for all that are in authority." Godliness and honesty are pretty good byproducts of good leadership, but we don't see as much of that now. Perhaps it is because God's people are not praying. Regardless of your political affiliation and/or your stance on governments throughout the world, yield your members over to God for Him to influence your voting, your talk, and your prayer life. Don't whine and complain, pray and believe God will put the right people in the right places at the right time for our good. You matter...your prayers matter... do what matters...

Prayer

Heavenly Father, I lift up every local, state, and federal official and ask You place Godly men and women in positions of authority. Order the steps of our great nation and help us to operate in Godly principles so we are able to live quiet and peaceable lives. I pray that Your hand guide the hearts of kings throughout every nation and tribe and help us all live at peace with one another. I ask for your blessings on my finances and that you bless every gift, offering, and tax I pay so my provisions serve Your Kingdom purposes in my life, in our government, and in the Church. Holy Spirit, come have your way in the lives of all leaders in this land and remove those who do not serve the greater good and honor the God of all creation. Thank you for peace and wisdom to live well and live free. Amen.

CONQUER YOURSELF

"*I am very happy*
Because I have conquered myself
And not the world.
I am very happy
Because I have loved the world
And not myself."

— SRI CHINMOY

"*Mortals make elaborate plans, but God has the last word.*
Humans are satisfied with whatever looks good; God probes
for what is good. Put God in charge of your work, then what
you've planned will take place. God made everything with a
place and purpose; even the wicked are included—but for
judgment. God cares about honesty in the workplace; your
business is his business. Get wisdom—it's worth more than
money; choose insight over income every time. First pride,
then the crash— the bigger the ego, the harder the fall. It's
better to live humbly among the poor than to live it up
among the rich and famous. Appetite is an incentive to work;

hunger makes you work all the harder. Moderation is better
than muscle, self-control better than political power. Make
your motions and cast your votes, but God has the final say."

— PROVERBS 16:1-4, 11, 16, 18-19, 26, 32-33 MSG

I like this quote from Chinmoy because it deals with this idea of conquering self and loving the world. We are to love the people of the world, but not the ways of the world. Romans 12:2 reminds us that we are not to be conformed and Romans 8 tells us that friendship with the world is enmity with God. We are, however, to love God and love people. We must submit ourselves to God's will and purposes first and demonstrate self-control. This self-control helps us say "no" to the evil desires of the flesh. It also opens the door of our heart to learn how to put God in charge of our work and get His wisdom for our insights which is far more valuable than money. When we do this, we can love (agape - the God-kind of love) the world as we are supposed to. We have to love God, love ourselves, and love others. I believe that Jesus' commands in the New Testament make it clear when He teaches us to love our neighbor as ourselves. We should always put others first and consider their needs and how our gifts, talents, possessions and purpose may serve them. In order to be able to serve others well, we must be at peace with God and with who He has created us to be. The character of honesty and integrity must be shaped, diligence must be applied and wisdom must be employed. Pride will wreck our lives. Stoke the fires of good appetites because they inspire diligence. Moderation is the best muscle to build. It is discipline over self. Trust God. He has the final say. May his final say be, "Well done thou good and faithful servant." Servanthood, after all, is leadership. You will be very happy when you have conquered yourself and loved others.

Heavenly Father, I ask you to reveal to me Your plans and use me as your
ambassador. You promise in the book of James that any man who lacks wisdom
can ask of You and Your response is to give liberally without making us feel

ashamed of asking. I submit my will to Yours and ask that you give me the boldness and courage to live in moderation and demonstrate the fruit of self-control. Help me conquer self so I may benefit others through a testimony that pleases You. My heart is to do Your will and bring glory to Your name. Have Your way in my heart, mind, and life and do what is pleasing in your sight! It is in Jesus' name I pray. Amen.

BE PRESENT IN THE PRESENT

"The future is purchased by the present."

— SAMUEL JOHNSON

"Give your entire attention to what God is doing right now, and
don't get worked up about what may or may not happen
tomorrow. God will help you deal with whatever hard
things come up when the time comes."

— MATTHEW 6:34 MSG

There are many things that could be shared about living in the present. As a parent of four children (one engaged, one in college, one in high school and one in middle school) I am in a mode as a parent that requires I start intentionally letting go and letting them decide who they will be. As an influencer in their lives, I know the greatest impact I can have is the joy and diligence I exhibit before them daily. The greatest principle I understand in the Bible that applies to everything in life is the "seed and sower." The parable of the sower is one place we find this principle, but we also find in throughout the Bible as we see scriptures about sowing and reaping and scriptures about storing up treasure in heaven, give and it shall be given, etc.

We have no control over time, but we do have control in how we utilize that time that is currently at our disposal. We can't get ready for a marathon in one week, but we can run more today than yesterday or do something differently today that impacts our tomorrow. Lesson 1 from the principle of the seed is that I can only plant now. I can't plant a better yesterday. I can't plant a better tomorrow, but I can plant better today for a better tomorrow that will impact how I feel about my yesterdays. Lesson 2 is to trust God with your work. Seek first the Kingdom... If we do everything we do as unto the Lord, we truly have an advocate and caretaker willing to help us get more out of this life than we could on our own. We quote, "I can do all things...", but we often forget that it's in a context that Paul is talking about knowing how to be content when he is abounding and suffering, when he's full and when he's in need. We have to believe that we are more than we can see at the moment while, at the same time, strive to see more through vision and through dreaming.

Without a dream we perish. The farmer plants today so he can harvest in the fall. We can't just work today, mindless of tomorrow, but we can't let worry and thought about tomorrow cripple our acts today. Seek God and simply do what you can today and know that tomorrow will be taken care of by your Father who is a far better father than you or I. Don't worry, be active! Actively pursue your purposeful living and God will direct your paths. Let His Word be a lamp and light. When you don't know what to do, do the best thing you do know and let God handle the working it out! The last idea about a seed that I will mention is that a seed has all potential within itself to reproduce what it is designed for. You can count on good seed producing good fruit. It may not be immediate, but all that is needed for new life is in a seemingly dead seed. When it's put into the right environment to live and tended to, it produces in magnitude much greater than its beginning.

Heavenly Father, You command us to avoid worry and to trust that our seeking Your Kingdom first positions us for having our basic needs met. Help me to be faithful in the present circumstances I face and to believe in my heart that you are ordering my steps to keep me in the center of Your will. I will hide Your Word in my heart so that I will not sin against You and trust that the seed of your Word will produce good fruit in my life. Come Holy Spirit and nourish, water, and take care of the seed in my heart so that my life is principled and purposeful. In Jesus' name I pray, Amen.

CONCLUSION

The most basic and fundamental responsibility we have as humans is to demonstrate rulership over the domain God has granted us. We can't rule out of greatness or because of our power and control, but we have the right to dominate the inhumane substances that surround us. We don't get to dominate people. People have to willingly submit. Leadership is the influence that will cause folks to be willing to submit. Can you influence yourself to become the best version of you possible? Can you influence others to strive for excellence by the way you live your life? There are certain characteristics good leaders are able to demonstrate. May you endeavor to courageously live and take on, moment by moment, each challenge that presents itself with the mindset of a conqueror who is committed to finish well. May your life be rightly fueled by passion to live on purpose based on principles that are timeless and self-evident. Respect yourself, others, and your surrounding environment so you maximize your potential to live responsibly on the side of the right. Give CPR to the heart of your leadership journey by developing each of these characteristics in your life and pressing into the challenges you face.

LIVE LIFE LOUD so your expression of the daily walk shows up loud and proud. Develop a vision demanding integrity, worthy of intentional faithfulness you can execute. Love and serve others in such a way that only God could build such bridges. Live a spirit led life through consistently feeding the soul and crucifying the flesh. Your best life is ahead if you are willing to invest yourself wholly in becoming yourself so you may benefit others. Nurture this heart of a champion so your life is loud and your discipleship is evident. Run to obtain the prize, discipline yourself, and you will hear the Father say, "Well done, my good and faithful servant (Matthew 25:21 KJV.)"

AFTERWORD

We live in a world that is rapidly changing. There are many great strengths in our up and coming leaders such as their desire for authenticity and transparency. This new generation is able to access unbelievable amounts of information at the touch of a screen. The Information Age has evolved into the knowledge-worker age; however, much of the knowledge is not managed with an effective filter of virtuous character to ensure its appropriate application. Just because we know more does not necessarily mean we are doing more with what we know. Knowledge can be extremely beneficial, but it can also distract and harm when it is not utilized intentionally within a framework of vision and integrity that demands effective execution. Some of the challenges we face in building this next generation of leaders, according to Tim Elmore in his [1]book, *Marching Off the Map: Inspire Students to Navigate a Brand New World*, are as follows:

Ubiquitous technology – we use it everywhere.

Pluralistic ideology – we buy into almost anything.

Addictive pathology – we can't cope without something.

Superficial theology – we believe in nearly everything.

Artificial methodology – we seek virtual answers from anywhere (p.38.)

Does this sound familiar? We are navigating a time where we must balance the dichotomy of faith in the up and coming potential for greatness and concern over the foundational principles guiding the next generation of leaders. I have served as a teacher, coach, administrator, and church volunteer for the past 25 years and I am disheartened yet excited, anxious yet energized, cautious yet courageous, and committed to see us conquer. It is my hope this book holds valuable knowledge and truths that can be found consistently throughout the most fundamental observations of nature. I hope the principles found in the acronyms housed in C.P.R., L.I.V.E. L.I.F.E. L.O.U.D., and B.E.S.T. will resonate in the hearts and minds of leaders and serve as a sort of lighthouse or stake driven in the ground holding us steady while the winds of change blow all around us. The most important parts of any structure are the foundational underpinnings and structural frameworks that support and protect the valuable furnishings inside. May we all seek to build a strong structural framework of leadership integrity in our own lives so we are not blown around by every wind of change and confused by the plethora of information (misinformation) seeking to aid us in our transformation. May we be transformed by the renewing of our minds by His Word and truth consistent with the Word of God so our lives are proof it pays to listen and obey. Don't be blown around by every wind of doctrine and fancy catch phrases that are not rooted in principles. Develop the character of C.P.R. in the heart of a champion. Run your race and LIVE LIFE LOUD. Be spirit led, soul fed, and body dead in your pursuit as a disciple or follower of truth. Take responsibility for your own improvement and the improvement of the organizations you lead by choosing to FIX IT. Discipline to devote yourself daily to learning and growing so you are prepared to be a diligent doer of what is right and your testimony will help others to overcome. Lead people to do things that matter.

NOTES

3. THE THREE C'S: COURAGE, COMMITMENT, AND CONQUEROR

1. Rutland, Mark. *Hanging by a Thread.* Lake Mary, FL.: Creation House, 1992.
2. Carnegie, Dale *How to Win Friends and Influence People.* New York: Simon & Schuster, 1981.

5. THE THREE R'S: RESPECT, RESPONSIBILITY, RIGHT

1. Willink, Jocko and Leif, Babin. 2017. *Extreme Ownership: How U.S. Navy SEALs Lead and Win.* New York: St. Martin's Press, 49.

6. LEAD WITH INTEGRITY AROUND A VISION FOR EXCELLENCE!

1. Covey, Stephen R. 2004. *The 8th Habit: From Effectiveness to Greatness.* New York: Free Press.

7. LIVE WITH INTENT AND FAITHFULNESS TOWARD EXECUTION!

1. McChesney, Chris, Sean Covey, and Jim Huling. 2012. *The 4 Disciplines of Execution: Achieving Your Wildly Important Goals*

9. THE TRINITY OF MAN: INTEGRATION OF SPIRIT, SOUL, AND BODY

1. Wuest, Kenneth Samuel. *The New Testament: an Expanded Translation.* Eerdmans, 1994.
2. Peshawaria, Rajeev. *"Trust: The Currency Of Leadership."* Forbes. Forbes Magazine, September 23, 2013. https://www.forbes.com/sites/rajeevpeshawaria/2013/09/22/trust-the-currency-of-leadership/#26797c5179eb.

11. LIFE APPLICATION: SPRING CLEANING

1. Collins, Jim. *Good to Great Why Some Companies Make the Leap... and Others Don't*. New York, NY: HarperBusiness, 2001.

AFTERWORD

1. Elmore, Tim and Andrew. McPeak. Marching Off the Map: Inspire Students to Navigate a Brand New World. Atlanta, Georgia.

ABOUT DONALD PAUL WILDER

Paul Wilder grew up in South Georgia where he excelled in running and accepted an athletic scholarship to attend Berry College where he met Amy. Paul and Amy have both been in the teaching profession for over 25 years. They have worked to raise their own four children (Caleb, Natalie, Joshua, Timothy) and served other families in raising their children as well. Paul has been a teacher and coach, administrator, church volunteer, and church leader alongside his role as husband and father. His desire to write this book hinges on his desire to "lead people to do things that matter."

For more information, visit www.DPaulWilder.com

CPSIA information can be obtained
at www.ICGtesting.com
Printed in the USA
LVHW022314060421
683674LV00017B/1135